From Carrigdrumruske to Carrick-on-Shannon

Maynooth Studies in Local History

SERIES EDITOR Michael Potterton

The six volumes in the MSLH series for 2024 cover a broad chronological and geographical canvas across four provinces, focusing variously on people, places, families, communities and events. It begins with an unlikely search for Vikings in the north-west of Ireland, where the evidence is more compelling than most people realize. Further south, in Carrick-on-Shannon, we trace the fortunes of the St George family from the Plantation of Leitrim through to the decades after the Famine. From Carrick we continue south to Ballymurray in Roscommon and its Quaker community (1717–1848), including their relationship with the Croftons of Mote Park. Further south still, in 1701 Jacobite Patrick Hurly of Moughna, Co. Clare, was at the centre of a 'sham robbery' of gold and jewellery worth about €500,000 in today's money. Unlike Hurly, Mary Mercer was renowned for her charitable endeavours, including the establishment of a shelter for orphaned girls in Dublin three hundred years ago in 1724. Finally, the last volume in this year's crop examines the evolution of the resilient farming community at Carbury in Co. Kildare.

* * *

Raymond Gillespie passed away after a very short illness on 8 February 2024. He had established the Maynooth Studies in Local History (MSLH) series with Irish Academic Press in 1995, from which time he served as series editor for a remarkable 27 years and 153 volumes. Taking over those editorial reins in 2021, my trepidation was tempered by the knowledge that Raymond agreed to remain as an advisor. True to his word, he continued to recommend contributors, provide peer-review, mentor first-time authors (and series editors) and give sound advice. Shoes that seemed big to fill in 2021 just got a lot bigger.

Maynooth Studies in Local History: Number 168

From Carrigdrumruske to Carrick-on-Shannon: the St George estate, 1613–1864

Mairead Lynch

FOUR COURTS PRESS

Set in 11.5pt on 13.5pt Bembo by
Carrigboy Typesetting Services for
FOUR COURTS PRESS LTD
7 Malpas Street, Dublin 8, Ireland
www.fourcourtspress.ie
and in North America for
FOUR COURTS PRESS
c/o IPG, 814 N Franklin Street, Chicago, IL 60610

ISBN 978-1-80151-131-5

Printed in Ireland
by Sprint Books, Dublin

Contents

Acknowledgments

I would like to express my sincere thanks to Michael Potterton for inviting me to contribute to this series and for his support and encouragement throughout this experience. I am most grateful to Brendan Scott for his invaluable advice and for sharing his vast knowledge of Leitrim. I am particularly indebted to the late Raymond Gillespie who so generously gave his time, expertise and support and reminded me of the importance of telling a story. I cannot fail to mention Derek Barter and his colleagues in the Department of Adult and Community Education, Maynooth University, for delivering a truly inspirational BA degree programme that rekindled my interest in local history.

I would like to thank the archivists and librarians at the National Library of Ireland, the staffs at the Local Studies Department of Leitrim County Library, the National Archives of Ireland and the John Paul II Library, Maynooth, all of whom enthusiastically facilitated my research. I am especially grateful to my friends Bríd Nolan and Jackie Lacey who read my initial drafts and provided gentle guidance and encouragement. I would also like to thank my friends Deirdre Gleeson and Jackie Horan and all those who patiently listened and gave their support.

My greatest debt of gratitude is due to my husband Jim and my daughters Aoife and Ciara who, despite concerns that I had abandoned the present for the past, were always there when I needed them.

I am extremely grateful to photographer Mark Kelly who allowed me access to his exceptional photographic collection. His beautiful picture of Carrick Bridge, featured on the front cover, wholly encapsulates the journey from Carrigdrumruske to Carrick-on-Shannon.

Introduction

Carrick-on-Shannon, the principal town and administrative centre of Co. Leitrim, is located in the southern part of the county on the main Dublin to Sligo road. It is situated on the banks of the River Shannon and is connected by a five-arched bridge to the neighbouring county of Roscommon (figs 1, 2). Once part of the Gaelic territory of West Bréifne, the borough town of Carrigdrumruske, later Carrickdrumrusk, was incorporated by royal charter in 1613.[1] By 1623, it was in the possession of plantation grantee George St George of Cambridgeshire and was an integral part of his Co. Leitrim estate. The borough's strategic position at a fording point of the Shannon dictated its location and form but, despite being rooted in war, dispossession and hardship, by the mid-nineteenth century it had emerged with 'the desirable appendages of a well-regulated town'.[2] Among its 'many agreeable features' were a thriving market, handsome public buildings, good houses, large shops and a quay for the convenience of a steamboat plying daily from Athlone.[3] Completing the picture, a promenade and pleasure grounds, 'for the recreation and amusement of the inhabitants', extended along the riverbank overlooked by the 'elegant mansion of Charles M. St George esq., the lord of the soil'.[4]

This is the story of an estate that by 1666 extended to more than 9,000 plantation acres[5] in Cos Leitrim and Roscommon. It charts the lives and times of the St George family as they built a dynasty upon those acres and played their part in creating a legacy that has stood the test of time. It explores how military prowess and political acuity facilitated an upwards trajectory in terms of their wealth, power and status. In addition, their chameleon-like ability to curry favour with the dominant power is examined alongside their sometimes questionable use of the authority it engendered. The extent to which the family may have become victims of the institutions they helped to create is also considered and the repercussions for the town and estate are assessed. The St Georges' part in the anglicization,

1. Map of Co. Leitrim from Bernard Scalé, *An Hibernian atlas; or,
General description of the kingdom of Ireland* (London, 1776)

2. Map of Co. Roscommon from Scalé, *An Hibernian atlas* commercialization and physical development of the area is studied in conjunction with the outcomes experienced by the native and Old English inhabitants and settlers introduced from Britain. Across all sectors there were losses and gains. The native Irish suffered hugely but for some the removal of traditional constraints created opportunities that proved difficult to resist. The actions and reactions of the different social groups are explored over time revealing the survival strategies adopted by a volatile community that was separated by religion and ethnicity but bound together by economic dependence and an attachment to a place that was home. The last St George to own the estate died in 1864 and in 1923 the estate passed to the Land Commission. The town of Carrick-on-Shannon (henceforth Carrick) stands in testimony to the St George family and the multiple generations of inhabitants who helped steer its course.

This study is divided into four parts. The first chapter examines the St Georges' role in Ireland's conquest and colonization and their acquisition of the strategically positioned Carrick estate as a reward. The second chapter discusses how, having built a dynasty and acquired the means of creating a legacy, the St Georges struggled with financial commitments, premature death and the failure of the immediate male line. Their attempts to secure the dynasty and protect their individual interests are examined in the context of the degeneration of the estate and the enforced sale of over seven thousand acres. In Chapter 3, the rise of the Catholic community is explored relative to the St Georges' absence, the relaxation of the Penal Laws and the impact of the 1798 Rebellion. The town continued to evolve and expand but responsibility for its development is shown to have rested largely on a group of middle-class inhabitants whose religious and political differences were pushing them further apart. The last chapter examines the complex social adjustment that accompanied Charles St George's intermittent residency and the disastrous consequences of the Great Irish Famine. As the country experienced a crisis of unprecedented proportions, St George and the inhabitants of his estate were about to face their final test.

No detailed study of Carrick town or estate exists. Robert O'Byrne's history of Tyrone House, Co. Galway, is the only published source dedicated to the family.[6] Works by Gerard MacAtasney and Liam Kelly and compilations of interdisciplinary essays covering Cos Leitrim and Roscommon[7] are a valuable source of information in relation to the counties in general and provide some specific details of Carrick town and its environs. Throughout this study, material relating specifically to the Carrick estate is derived mainly from evidence gathered in respect of legal disputes argued *c*.1728 and *c*.1790, an estate survey completed in 1768 and rentals and accounts covering the period 1842–71.[8] Examination of the patent rolls, 1641 depositions, books of survey and distribution and a 1749 survey of the diocese of Elphin[9] allow the details extracted from early rental fragments to be coordinated and expanded. In addition, official reports and enquiries, the archival records of the dukes of Ormond, newspapers, maps and travellers' reviews contribute to a better understanding of the people, the place and the times. It is, however, important to stress that all primary sources used in this study were produced in a specific context, almost all were written in English by well-educated authors and they are unlikely to have represented the community as a whole. As a person's position in the social hierarchy generally dictated the permitted strength of their voice, a significant proportion of the estate's population most likely went unheard. In 1812, Edward Wakefield estimated that Leitrim's Catholic inhabitants outnumbered their Protestant counterparts by ratio of 30:1. Notwithstanding this statistic, Catholics, he observed 'possess the greater part of personal property; but they are individually too poor to have political interest, therefore their influence is of no importance'.[10] It is not possible to reinstate their voices but it is hoped that in highlighting the absence, the sound of their silence might be heard.

1. Creating the legacy, 1603–91

In May 1600, a fleet of warships sailed up the River Foyle carrying four thousand soldiers to reinforce the crown's hitherto unsuccessful assault on Hugh O'Neill, earl of Tyrone (c.1550–1616).[1] Included among their numbers was 22-year-old William St George, eldest son of Richard St George of Hatley St George in Cambridgeshire, England. William, as recorded by his father, was 'slayne at Lafoyle' within weeks of his arrival.[2] In October the same year, William's brother John was mortally wounded by Tyrone's forces and was laid to rest in Dundalk.[3] A third member of the family, most likely their younger brother George, was 'shot in the shoulder but not to death'.[4] Like many young men of their ilk, the St Georges most likely prided themselves on being part of a fighting class whose service on the battlefield was a measure of their virtue.[5] Being members of 'an ancient but somewhat reduced family', they could support an elite birthright but lacked the wealth needed to progress their social standing.[6] For the St Georges, therefore, the war in Ireland represented an opportunity to achieve honour on the battlefield and take advantage of the rewards that were afforded. Tyrone surrendered in 1603, following which the lord deputy, Charles Blount, 8th Baron Mountjoy (1563–1606), informed the new king, James I (1566–1625), that 'this kingdom is now made capable of what form it shall please the king to give it'.[7] The conquest of Ireland was complete. George St George, having played his part in Tyrone's downfall, was aptly positioned to participate in the reengineering of Irish society and to secure a favourable position in the new social and political hierarchy.

CARRICK TOWN AND ESTATE

In March 1603 Mountjoy turned his attention to Co. Leitrim. Situated on the eastern edge of Connacht, bordered by Ulster and Leinster and transected by the River Shannon, possession of this strategically positioned territory was essential if an affordable domination of Ireland was to be achieved.[8] Described as a 'wild and unhaunted wasteness', the county was said to have 'neither ancient nor new English' and a population of seditious 'firebrands' who were 'first out in action and last in submission'.[9] The O'Rourkes dominated the north of the county while their MacRannall under-lords controlled Muintir Eolais, an area roughly coterminous with the barony of Leitrim. By 1605, the O'Rourkes had been outmanoeuvred and a British plantation was considered an 'absolute necessity'.[10] It was suggested that the leaderless population would be amenable to crown intervention, allowing a plantation to be implemented 'without charge or fear of danger'.[11] In preparation, a castle was constructed at *Cora Droma Rúisc* ('weir of the ridge of the marsh') and in March 1613 the borough of Carrigdrumruske was incorporated, with power to elect two members of parliament.[12] By comparison, Co. Roscommon was a product of the fluctuating balance of power and cross-cultural assimilation that existed between its Irish, Anglo-Norman and New English inhabitants.[13] Being 'more within command', the need for a crown-controlled colonization was viewed with less urgency than that afforded its volatile neighbour.[14]

In July 1616 George St George's chances of advancement were increased by the appointment of his uncle Oliver St John, later Viscount Grandison (1559–1630), to the office of Ireland's lord deputy.[15] The following September, St George was granted lands in Tyrone, Fermanagh and Cavan.[16] His fortunes were further enhanced when, in 1619, title to the disputed territory of Leitrim was settled in favour of the crown. In October 1620, while Brian O'Rourke, the displaced heir, was incarcerated in a London prison, plans for the county's plantation were ratified. By February 1621, the lord deputy confirmed that, 'glad to relinquish the old insolent … title of O'Rourke', the whole of Leitrim had 'freely submitted themselves'.[17] Fifty per cent of all viable land was to be granted to British undertakers. Natives were promised three-quarters of their original holdings subject to a maximum of one thousand acres. 'Inferior natives', holders of less than one hundred acres, were to receive leases in lieu of their freehold interests.[18] With plantation grants at the lord deputy's discretion, forty-six undertakers received relatively fertile holdings in frontier positions, providing a barrier between Leitrim

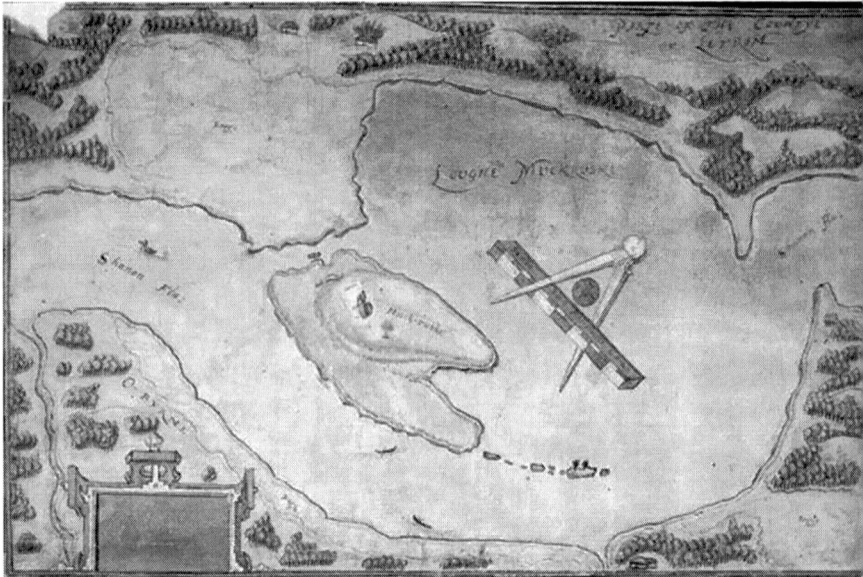

3. Island of Muckruske, *c.*1602, by Richard Bartlett (MS 2656,12)
(reproduced courtesy of the National Library of Ireland)

and surrounding counties. St John's nephew George received 400
acres close to the newly incorporated borough of Carrigdrumruske.
Prior to completion of the plantation negotiations, St George was
also granted reversionary title to 'Drumruske' castle, which was
held by Sir Maurice Griffith 'at the yearly rent of 40*s*. Irish'.[19] By
July 1623, Griffith had been ousted and St George had procured full
possession.[20] The castle lands included the 'island of Inishunckar',
which was possibly the former O'Rourke 'fortress of Inchmucker'.[21]
Attesting to the strategic importance of this small island, it was
excluded from the grant of 'O'Rowrke's country' made to Teige
O'Rourke in 1604 and was instead retained by the crown 'for defence
of the kingdom'.[22] The island was most likely the focus of military
cartographer Richard Bartlett's representation of Lough Muckrusk,
depicted *c.*1602 (fig. 3). The castle grant also included a swathe of
land bordering the Shannon, which encompassed the borough of
Carrick. The borough was administered by an exclusively Protestant
corporation headed by an annually elected provost.[23] The corporation
was responsible for the making of by-laws, the provision of a small-

claims court and the management of markets, fairs and tolls. It also directed the appointment of town officials and the election of two members of parliament.[24] St George, as owner of the town, controlled the corporation and the functions within its remit. He also enjoyed exclusive rights to the Shannon and Boyle rivers within ten kilometres either side of the castle.[25] By November 1633, at a cost of £100, St George had constructed a bridge over the Shannon and petitioned Charles I for the right to collect tolls in respect of all 'cattle and other carriages' using the crossing.[26] This request and patent for a second fair were granted, subject to an annual fee of £20. By 1641, St George was in possession of almost 1,800 acres extending along the banks of the Shannon for approximately 2km either side of Carrick.[27] Five kilometres downriver, Charles Coote received £3,000 to develop and fortify the town of Jamestown.[28] Together they controlled Shannon navigation and access to Connacht.

In Roscommon, the principal landholders included the McDermotts, Mulloys, Kellys, Plunketts and newcomers the Kings of Boyle.[29] With the threat of plantation looming, Gaelic and Old English inhabitants struggled to secure their holdings and vied with new English immigrants. Between 1600 and 1641 the population of Ireland grew from around 1.4 million to approximately 2.1 million. The labour force increased accordingly and with surplus outputs fuelling an expanding market-based economy, wealthy merchants and speculators took advantage of the uncertain land market.[30] By 1641, 20 per cent of Roscommon land was in English hands and St George had acquired just over 1,200 acres in the county, much of which bordered the Shannon adjacent to his Leitrim holding.[31] The fair green was positioned on the western side of the river providing economic foci in both counties and increased tolls on the bridge.[32] It is unclear where the St Georges maintained a residence, but evidence suggests that having initially lived in the castle the family home was later sited in the current townland of Hartley, approximately 1.5km upriver from Carrick. Estate maps produced in 1768 depict a large house occupying a 122-acre site in an area then known as Corsparrow. Denoted as Hatley Manor, its emulation of the ancestral home at Hatley St George in Cambridgeshire supports the likelihood of it being the St George residence. In 1836, during the Ordnance Survey's mapping of Ireland, Hatley was construed as a misspelling of the family name Hartley. The St Georges' attempt to inscribe their Cambridgeshire origins in the place-name record was lost in translation and Hartley became the official name of the townland.[33]

In June 1622, a Commission of Enquiry was set up to consider the state of Irish affairs.[34] The ramifications of the Leitrim Plantation were scrutinized and it was revealed that instructions had largely been ignored or abused.[35] Whereas grants were to be made to 151 natives, many lost more than a quarter of their original acreage or were unfairly treated 'for the quality of their assignations'.[36] Other native freeholders, having 'by measurement [been] found under rate', failed to meet the criteria required to receive a grant of title. Along with 'inferior natives' they were 'turned out of their lands' and, in the absence of the promised lease, were effectively dispossessed.[37] This latter situation was exacerbated by the increased subdivision of land that, despite legislation to the contrary, was a consequence of the growing population and the continued adherence to the partible inheritance practice known as gavelkind. In addition to the abuses perpetrated by plantation administrators, many native inhabitants were disadvantaged by the self-serving actions of their better-informed English-speaking kinsmen.[38] Evidencing the corrupt implementation of the plantation process, Melaghlin MacRannall, the former holder of Corsparrow, was allocated a shared leasehold interest in eighty-three acres near Mohill, which he most likely never received.[39] Whereas most Leitrim natives suffered to varying degrees, the plantation presented opportunities for collateral families whose lesser positions in the Gaelic hierarchy had restricted their chances of advancement. For some, like the MacRannalls of Muintir Eolais, the removal of the O'Rourkes and extension of British control allowed various members of the ancient family to participate in the new administration. A William Reynolds (anglicization) was MP for Leitrim in 1613, John Reynolds of Lough Scur was high sheriff from 1613 to 1620 and his son Humphrey held the position until 1624.[40] Consequently, having adapted to the new regime they were in a better position than most native inhabitants and fared well when it came to the allocation of land.

With a substantial landholding in his possession, George St George needed to supplement monies earned from the estate in order to maximize its potential and advance the economic status of the town. The army continued to offer career opportunities and the prospect of social advancement. He served as controller of ordnance and constable of the castle at Carrick and was commander of Grandison's company of foot.[41] St George also took an active role in the Connacht administration. In 1627, he replaced his uncle as vice-admiral of Connacht, a sinecure normally reserved for holders of high office.[42] Based at Carrick, he is believed to have been one of only two provincial holders to have ever resided permanently within their jurisdiction. Between 1628 and 1638, with policing of officials on the western seaboard presenting difficulties for the admiralty, St George was required to account for the suspiciously low returns which resulted in an average annual profit of only £15, earned from just one seized ship and several beached whales.[43] Beyond the contentious financial benefits associated with the position, the role afforded considerable status and enabled St George to curry favour with 'divers nobles', whom he plied with 'chests of sugar' and exotic spoils.[44] Moneylending also provided a lucrative means of investing surplus cash and creating economic dependencies. The St Georges earned interest on their outlay and exercised their possessory right to mortgaged properties in the event of debtor default. Lands acquired in this manner included the townland of Clogher in Co. Roscommon upon which the earl of Westmeath had secured a loan of £330.[45] In addition, legally registered debts and associated securities formed part of the financial negotiations that preceded the brokering of appropriate marriages.[46] The St Georges also used their control of Carrick corporation to instigate and further their political careers. Sir George represented the borough from 1639 to 1649 and the seat was occupied by various members of the family until it was sold to the Clements family in 1756.[47]

George and his wife Katherine had eleven children, seven of whom survived to adulthood. Their marriages enabled St George to forge connections with an established network of New English elite, which, combined with the career advantages engendered by his uncle, Viscount Grandison, enabled him to further his influence in Connacht society. His children were similarly prolific, ensuring a viable bloodline and allowing the family's sphere of influence to be further extended through increasingly strategic alliances (appendix 1). On 5 August 1627 St George was dubbed a knight of

the realm and, asserting his association with Carrick, he assumed
the title Sir George St George of Carrickdrumrusk.[48] His elevation
coincided with a proliferation of creations designed to provide
revenue and an inexpensive means of controlling the kingdom. It
also marked the beginning of the family's social ascent and cemented
their participation in a social engineering process which would have
a profound impact on the physical and cultural landscape of Carrick.

REBELLION AND CIVIL WAR

In February 1641, professing a desire to encourage industry and
allegiance, the gentlemen of Leitrim petitioned the House of
Commons to remove the restrictions preventing patentees from
selling lands to the 'mere Irish'.[49] Whether oblivious to the rising
disquiet or anxious to dispose of their holdings, their optimism was
misplaced. Gaelic tenant farmers who were the mainstay of plantation
estates, as opposed to being in a position to purchase land, were
struggling to meet their commitments and resented being financially
indebted to their settler neighbours.[50] Dispossession, dislocation and
impoverishment, compounded by religious differences, embittered
a native population who would 'rather choose to die in rebellion'
than live under a government that had taken their land 'upon bare
pretences or obscure titles'.[51] On 22 October, the 1641 Rebellion
began in the neighbouring province of Ulster. The following day
the rising had spread to Leitrim where robberies were reported in the
parish of Kiltoghert.[52] Four days later Roscommon was embroiled
in the fray as 'great numbers of rebellious Irish' seized property in
the barony of Boyle.[53] By November, the lords justices declared that
multitudes of rebels making 'religion part of their pretences' had
'seized the houses and estates of almost all the English ... in Leitrim'
and gained a foothold in Roscommon.[54] In December 1641, Brian
O'Rourke, the last lord of Leitrim, died in the Tower of London,
adding fuel to the fire.[55]

As the situation escalated, in Leitrim the O'Rourkes and
MacRannalls commanded an organized military campaign with
local farmers, like the McKeons of Kiltoghert, making up its rank
and file. In attempt to maintain order and legitimize their actions,

they mimicked the mechanisms of royal authority, appointing their own justices of peace, sheriffs and a legal adviser whom they styled 'the king's attorney'.[56] The Leitrim insurrectionists were joined by the McDermotts, Kellys and Mulloys, the 'cheefe rebells' of Co. Roscommon. Brian O'Beirne of Dangan, a former army captain employed by the lord president of Connacht, had switched sides and was reputedly tyrannizing the Protestant inhabitants of Carrick and Jamestown.[57] Following the defection of the lords of Pale, the Roscommon insurgents were joined by the Dillons and Brabazons and 'others of the gentrie of the county', their involvement motivated by distrust of the Dublin government and the perceived threat to the Catholic landed interest.[58] In 1637, St George received a revised patent in respect of all lands which comprised the Carrick estate. The grant included the castle but was subject to a provision allowing the crown to 'make a garrison thereof in any time of war or commotion'.[59] With the castle at the king's disposal, St George, Charles Coote the younger and Captain King of Boyle marshalled the crown forces under their command and marched through Leitrim and Roscommon determined to 'burne and spoyle all about them'.[60] In north Leitrim, Sir Frederick Hamilton of Manorhamilton (1590–1647) supplemented the standing army under his control, attacked Irish encampments and claimed to have killed up to 1,200 insurgents and civilians.[61] Notwithstanding the actions of ambitious military officers, most settlers kept a low profile and sought refuge in nearby garrisons. While St George and Coote were occupied in Roscommon, Jamestown was besieged by a company of rebels led by the O'Rourkes. The occupants of Carrick and Jamestown garrisons were reduced to near starvation and, as deposed by the local parson, lost sixty inhabitants to rebel attack. The deceased included twelve persons with Irish surnames, Sergeant Harrison who commanded Carrick fort and a young child who was taken from her Irish nurse at Jamestown and reputedly thrown against a tree.[62]

In May 1642 the Confederate Catholics of Ireland, an oath-bound association of Irish, Old English and some New English Catholics, established a quasi-parliament and a political nation defined by religion.[63] Ten assemblies of the Confederate Supreme Council took place in Kilkenny between 1641 and 1649. During this period the rebellion evolved into a protracted war fought between Confederate forces and a royal Irish army commanded by the marquis of Ormond (1610–88). In September 1643 a ceasefire was agreed.[64] St George complied with the truce but Coote continued to 'ravage' Roscommon where it was reported the inhabitants were 'universally incensed' against him.[65] While peace negotiations continued, fighting persisted with varying degrees of intensity and Leitrim and Roscommon were said to be experiencing 'great difficulties and distress'.[66] Due to their strategic positions, the garrisons at Carrick and Jamestown were a focus of rebel attention, placing the St George estate directly in the firing line. Whereas the forts provided asylum to English settlers fleeing rebel attack, the names of persons killed or associated with Jamestown suggest a degree of ethnic interaction that involved the employment or harbouring of native Irish, some of whom 'went to the Protestant church'.[67] Both forts surrendered to the Confederates in 1642, were recaptured by the Irish army but by 1648 were again in Catholic hands.[68] With truce negotiations causing a split in the Confederate camp, the anti-treaty army captured Carrick, while Jamestown remained loyal to the pro-treaty Confederation.[69]

Despite widespread allegations of plantation mismanagement, St George escaped without censure, while his contemporary, 'that humaine-bloudsucker' Charles Coote was accused of violent extortion.[70] Whereas St George had in 1622 been among the 92 per cent of undertakers said to 'never come upon the lands', his subsequent active, albeit self-interested, participation in the 'civilization' process differed from many of his contemporaries.[71] Improvements to the fort, construction of a bridge and successful operation of fairs and markets attest to the emergence of a functional economic hub servicing a developing agricultural hinterland. These changes, however, comprised 'that visible booty being the trumpett that proclaimed the warre'.[72] The Carrick estate, town and garrison most likely suffered during the insurrection but, despite the Coote family claiming to have made a substantial financial loss, there is no surviving record of damages incurred by the St Georges or persons known to have been associated with the estate.[73] As most of the witnesses deposed in the aftermath of the rebellion were Protestant, this deficit may be an indication of the extent of the estate's Catholic tenantry and the degree of displacement experienced by its settler community.[74] In February 1649, as Ireland embarked on a new phase in its turbulent history, around Carrick, the 'firebrands' were back in action, the O'Rourkes were again in control and St George was an officer in the army of a dethroned king.

THE CROMWELLIAN LAND SETTLEMENT

Following the execution of Charles I (1600–49), Ireland's Protestant and Catholic inhabitants were united in opposition to Oliver Cromwell (1599–1658) and his Commonwealth administration. Martial law was declared with its imposition directed by the armies of the Royalist alliance under the command of the marquis of Ormond. In Leitrim, the O'Rourkes held control while in Roscommon a consortium of Irish and Old English families shared the responsibility.[75] St George had followed Ormond's orders and adhered to the truce, but, mindful of Cromwell's military advantage, he switched sides. By June 1649, along with his eldest son Oliver, George commanded a regiment in Coote's Connacht forces and was an ardent supporter of parliament.[76] In September 1649, Cromwell landed in Ireland and by the following May, no match for his new model army, most eastern towns had capitulated.[77] At a meeting in Jamestown, the Catholic bishops declared Ormond accountable for the Irish annihilation and in December 1650 he joined the exiled Charles II in France.[78] Coote's parliamentarians besieged Athlone and Galway and took control of the Shannon.[79] In August 1651, with 'almost their whole strength in the kingdom' converging on Connacht, the new lord deputy, the marquis of Clanricarde (1604–57), retreated to the garrison at Carrick.[80] While St George's troops assaulted Clanricarde's patrimony, his fortress in Leitrim was the command centre of the struggling Royalist campaign. In October, as guerrilla warfare raged around Carrick, the lord deputy summoned an assembly at which it was resolved 'to stick firm to his majesty's government'.[81] In June 1652, however, the garrison was forced to surrender.[82] In August 1655 Coote's regiment was disbanded and St George and his son Oliver retained commissions in Ireland's new standing army under the command of Charles Coote, president of Connacht.[83]

Intent on restoring law and order and defraying wartime expenditure, Cromwell began the process of wresting power from Royalist landowners and vesting control in a new Protestant elite. In accordance with the Act of Settlement 1652, most Catholic landowners lost their estates and were relocated west of the Shannon.[84] Over eleven million acres of vacated land was made available to repay soldiers and adventurers who had fought or invested in the war.[85] Roscommon was one of four counties set aside to accommodate transplantees. Approximately 70 per cent of profitable land in the county was in Catholic hands and subject to forfeiture.[86] Charged with 'the better setting down of the transplantation', Coote enticed gentlemen of the Pale with descriptions of the 'plains of Boyle that fatten a bullock and a sheep to the acre'.[87] With Roscommon feted as a favourable proposition, transplanters from twenty-four counties were accommodated and only 27 per cent of resident Catholics retained land in the county.[88] Most were dispatched to the outer reaches of Mayo, Clare and Galway, while those allowed to remain lost the bulk of their land. The McDermotts, who held in excess of 13,000 acres, saw their holding reduced by 85 per cent.[89] St George and his sons qualified for arrears of pay and were also owed compensation for service prior to 1649. They took advantage of their roles in the process, reputedly accepting bribes, defrauding transplantees and purchasing decrees for as little as 2s. 6d. per acre, compared to £3 per acre specified by the 1642 Adventurers' Act.[90] In Leitrim, where only 39 per cent of land was held by Catholics, the impact of the Stuart plantation was apparent.[91] Considered 'a strong country', it was initially excluded from the settlement but subsequently overrun by nomadic Ulster herdsmen or Creaghts, the remaining Catholic land was appropriated for pre-1649 soldiery and native landholders were ordered to Murrisk and Borrishoole in Co. Mayo.[92]

Data extracted from the poll ordnances completed in 1660 reflects the relocation of Catholic landholders to Roscommon and the extent of Protestant occupation in the fertile barony of Boyle (table 1). The St Georges' incursion into the county, being most likely a work in progress, was yet to be documented. Over 92 per cent of Leitrim inhabitants were Irish, evidencing the volume of non-landed persons exempt from the settlement. Only eleven Irish title holders remained, compared to the 151 native grantees specified in 1620. In the neighbouring county of Longford, where a similar plantation had been implemented in 1619, of the forty-three freeholders recorded on creation of the county in 1570 only seventeen received grants and by 1660 only three title holders of native origin remained.[93] Demonstrating the failure of soldiers to occupy their lots, in Co. Leitrim there were only twenty-four Protestant title holders, many of whom had held lands since the plantation. Sir George and Lieut. Cunningham were the only title holders associated with Carrick town where, in 1660, the presence of just forty-seven tax-paying inhabitants suggests a lack of sustained development and a minimal presence at the garrison.[94]

Table 1. Estimated population of Leitrim and Roscommon, 1660

Location		Taxpayers		Title Holders	
Name	*Category*	*Irish*	*English*	*Irish*	*English*
Leitrim	County	3,956	319	11	24
Leitrim	Barony	823	155	3	9
Kiltoghert	Parish	434	147	2	9
Carrick	Town	14	33	0	2
Jamestown	Town	136	102	1	7
Corsparrow	Townland	9	2	0	0
Roscommon★	County	11,163	605	211	37
Boyle★	Barony	2,110	218	9	10
Boyle★	Town	256	142	0	4

(source: Pender (ed.), *Census of Ireland, c.1659*. ★figures include 89 soldiers and their wives stationed at Sir John King's garrison in Boyle town)

THE RESTORATION SETTLEMENT

Cromwell died in September 1658 and was succeeded by his ineffectual son, Richard. By the following June, the Commonwealth was in the throes of collapse and Ireland faced anarchy or military control.[95] In February 1660 a group of Protestants took over Dublin Castle and summoned a convention. Charles Coote jumped into action and, anxious to secure his position, Oliver St George followed suit. Coote and his officers proclaimed a 'full and free parliament', the elected members of which voted to reinstate the monarchy.[96] Charles

II's restoration occurred before the Cromwellian settlement had been
fully realized, leaving Protestants in possession of estates unable to
'shake off the apprehension of losing them', while Catholics who
had stuck firm to the royalist cause 'doe almost universally discourse
that they will have their lands agen'.[97] Protestants were united by
a common objective, but, intent on preserving their individual
interests, deep rivalries fomented. With the country experiencing a
period of relative peace, social and political connections were key but
fickle deciders in the battle for land and power. Oliver and his brother
George were prominent members of Coote's council, placing them in
pole position when it came to divvying out the spoils.

Oliver St George's part in restoring the monarchy secured him a
'free and general pardon'.[98] It also enhanced his social and political
standing and gave him access to the administrative tools that would
assist, albeit questionably, the acquisition of additional land. Having
been knighted by Henry Cromwell in February 1659, he was dubbed
again in July 1660 and in September the same year he was created
Baronet Oliver St George of Carrickdrumrusk.[99] Charles Coote
received the dignity of earl of Mountrath and his brother Richard,
who had married Oliver's sister Mary, was created Baron Coote
of Colooney.[100] In February 1660 Oliver was appointed to the
commission responsible for executing the settlement of Ireland, he
succeeded his father as vice-admiral of Connacht and in March 1661,
secured a position on the Council of Connacht.[101] It is estimated that
three out of every four soldiers granted land in lieu of pay chose
to liquidate their assets.[102] Many Irish Catholics were also forced to
sell. Described as 'the greediest man, advancing unjust use on unjust
use', Oliver St George made the most of the situation and reputedly
wrestled 'poor gentlemen out of their estates'.[103] In October 1666
Oliver was granted 3,096 acres in Roscommon, much of which had
been forfeit by the Plunkett and McDermott families. He also secured
3,112 acres in Limerick, 1,517 acres in Queen's County and 3,289 acres
at Headford, Co. Galway.[104] His brother George received 4,611 acres
in Dunmore and Ballymoe, Co. Galway.[105] Whereas the St George
family had profited hugely, some of their contemporaries fared even
better, with the Cootes' cumulative acquisitions exceeding 85,000
acres and the Kings of Boyle securing a massive 104,000 acres.[106]
Within two generations the St Georges' Carrick estate had grown

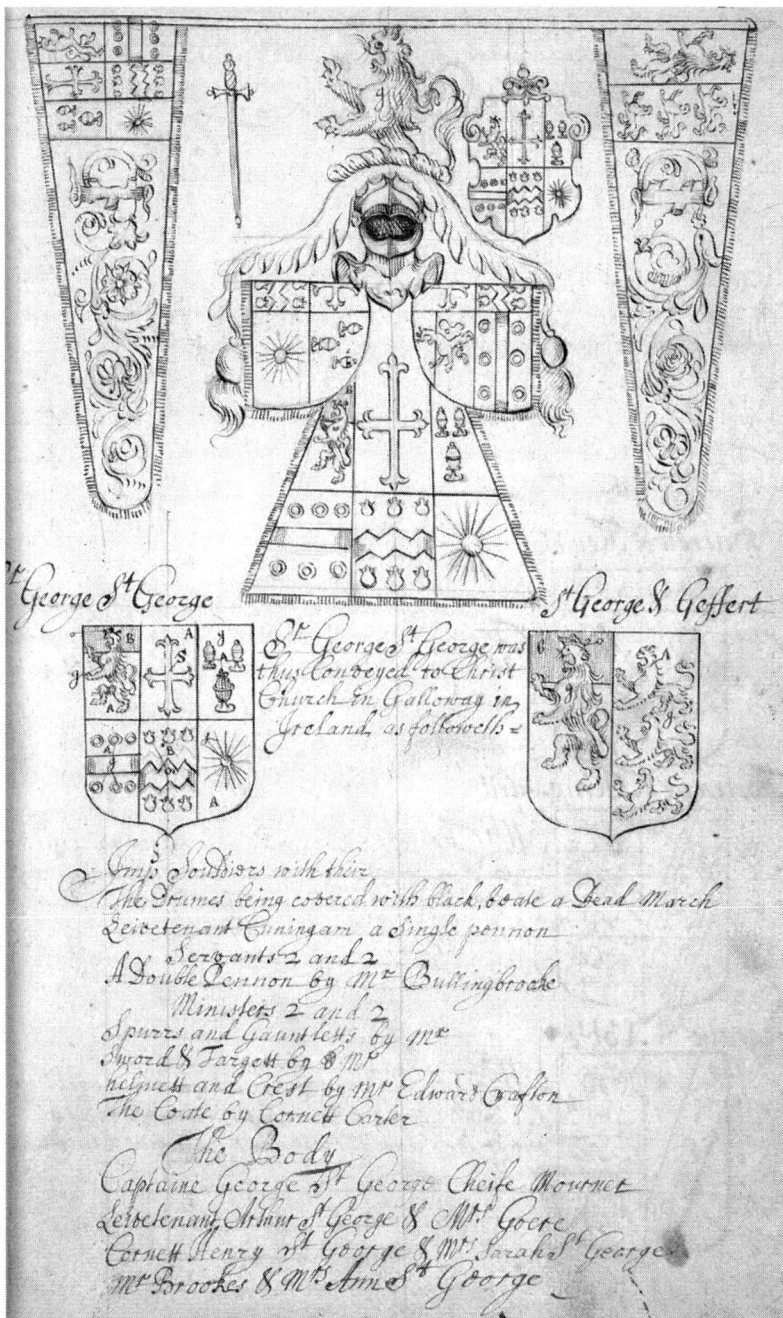

4. Funeral entry for Sir George St George, *c.*1661 (GO, MS 67)
(reproduced courtesy of the National Library of Ireland)

from 400 acres to approximately 6,600 acres in Cos. Leitrim and Roscommon. Acknowledging the family's Cambridgeshire origins, it was enrolled as the manor of Hatley St George but, testament to the influence of cross-cultural pragmatism, it remained known as the manor of Carrickdrumrusk.[107]

Sir George of Carrickdrumrusk died *c.*1661 and was interred at Christ Church in Galway town. His funeral highlighted the family's aristocratic origins and the extent of their newfound wealth and status (fig. 4). Whereas Baronet Oliver St George's choice of title honoured the family's Irish beginnings and Carrick's manorial designation paid homage to their English roots, Sir George's final resting place signalled an alignment with Co. Galway that would have significant repercussions in terms of the Carrick estate.

Throughout the 1660s political antagonism escalated. By August 1661, while the St Georges scrambled for land and fostered political connections, fears of another papist rebellion mounted.[108] The rebels, it was discovered, had devised a countrywide communication network that involved the interception of coded letters. In Leitrim, in order to allay suspicion, the letters were 'colourably' addressed to Lieut. Cunningham at Carrick garrison.[109] The unstable political climate prompted Ormond to increase the military presence at Carrick and treat with 'rebels and tories' in order to maintain the peace.[110] By June 1666, it was alleged that the rebels, having murdered and terrorized the king's subjects, had taken cover in the bogs around Carrick.[111] St George's troops were dispatched to hunt them down but failed to penetrate the hostile terrain.[112] By 1667, it was reported that Leitrim was 'unuseful to the king' and 'no fit place for an honest man to live in'.[113]

In addition to the social and monetary benefits of which Oliver St George undoubtedly availed, the exercising of his various administrative positions incurred specific responsibilities that were open to abuse, interpretation or censure. Lord Mountrath died in December 1661, leaving the St Georges without the support and direction of a major power broker whose ruthless ambition had furthered their social advancement. Oliver quickly aligned himself with the duke of Ormond who, in the uncertain political climate, relied on St George as a 'safe hand'.[114] In 1669 Ormond was removed from the lord lieutenancy and St George's position became increasingly tenuous. His dubious land deals were scrutinized and he was accused of stealing over £8,000 worth of cargo from an impounded ship.[115] Ormond used his influence to exonerate St George who covered all bases by cultivating the support of the new lord lieutenant, Arthur Capel, earl of Essex (1631–83). In November 1674 'the obliging Sir Oliver' was appointed to the Privy Council.[116] In the context of mounting anti-papist sentiment, St George was party to the council orders forbidding Catholics from carrying arms, banishing priests from the kingdom and preventing papists from living in all major towns.[117] Embroiled in the political hysteria, St George was implicated in events surrounding the execution of Oliver Plunkett and the fictitious Popish Plot. With the king in favour of 'turning him out of his employments', Ormond summoned him to Kilkenny where his years as a 'safe hand' may have influenced the outcome.[118] St George escaped with a reprimand, but the die had been cast and his reprieve was short-lived.

Despite constant skirmishing and mistrust at all levels of society, some semblance of a new normality began to emerge. War-torn lands were tilled and cattle trade with England began to thrive. The cattle acts of the 1660s, however, restricted the import of cheap Irish cattle into England and in Leitrim and Roscommon, as in most parts of Ireland, farmers were said to be 'broken', taxes remained uncollected and, compounded by a shortage of specie, arrears were paid in wheat.[119] St George's troops manned the magazine at Athlone, which functioned as a receiving depot for Connacht. Notwithstanding the reduction in the cattle trade, it is likely that the high levels of sheep farming associated with the barony of Boyle had a mitigating effect in terms of the Carrick estate. To counteract export restrictions, farmers began employing modern agricultural practices, producing goods for the European market. By the mid-1670s, Ireland had a buoyant agricultural economy and the numbers of Protestant settlers had begun to increase. The St Georges appear to have seized this opportunity and by 1681 a series of corn mills had been built at Mullaghatige, an area roughly coterminous with the current townlands of Lodge, Deerpark and Rock, approximately 5km from Carrick. A rental extract from May 1681 indicates an annual rental

income of £844 9s. 6d. earned from the Carrick estate.[120] Leases
had been issued to five English settlers who were resident in the
town, with the remainder of the town dwellers being tenants at
will. Beyond the town, the estate was divided into fifty agricultural
units with leases held by twelve specified tenants for periods of up
to twenty-one years (appendix 3). Rents were debited in respect of
the remaining properties, but no leases were issued and details of
individual tenancies were not recorded. Evidencing the complex
interdependencies that underpinned the new social order, on the
rural part of the estate, rents received from native or Old English
lessees amounted to £155 15s. compared to £129 9s. collected from
their settler counterparts. The estate's largest documented tenant was
a member of the Plunkett family whose kinsmen had been among
Roscommon's principal landholders prior to 1641. Their presence
demonstrates the St Georges' reliance on Catholic tenants and the
adaptions made by Gaelic and Old English inhabitants to survive on
their ancestral lands.[121] Despite the improved viability of the estate,
by 1683 Carrick town had just fourteen 'good houses' and compared
unfavourably with Jamestown which, being home to sixty families,
was considered the 'chief town in the county'.[122]

Whereas Oliver St George's administrative roles required an overt
involvement in the suppression of Catholics, religion was not a barrier
to his economic endeavours. During the 1670s, St George and Henry
McDermott Roe were said to have been joint owners of an iron
foundry at Ballyfarnan.[123] Economic pragmatism is also evidenced
by the extent of rental income derived from his Catholic tenantry.[124]
In terms of their cultural pursuits, the family also crossed the ethnic
divide. Written by the bard and composer Thomas Connellan
(c.1645–98) of Coloooney, Co. Sligo, *Molly St George* is the oldest
surviving harper-air with extant lyrics.[125] 'Maid Molly' was most
likely Oliver's sister Mary, Baroness Coote of Coloooney. Around
1684, Lady St George is credited with bringing the future harpist
Turlough O'Carolan to Carrick, where his father was offered work
in their foundry.[126] The St George's patronage came to an end with
accession of James II, following which support of the O'Carolans
passed to the McDermotts Roe.

THE WAR OF THE TWO KINGS

In February 1685, Charles II was succeeded by his Catholic brother
James II (1688–1701). Protestants, fearing that their already precarious
positions would be totally undermined, left the country in droves.
In April 1685, citing the 'long series of endeavours … by which he
strove to make reparation', Oliver St George begged forgiveness for
his Commonwealth sympathies and 'too easy belief' in the Popish
Plot.[127] His pleas fell on deaf ears, Oliver lost his army commission
and the St Georges departed for England. James II's promotion of
Catholicism and neutral European politics precipitated an invasion
by William of Orange (1650–1702). James left England in December
1688 and William and the king's daughter Mary (1662–94) assumed
control. Recognizing Ireland as a means of reconsolidating his
kingdom, in March 1689, James landed in Kinsale with assurance of
support from France. William, backed by Spain and the Holy Roman
Empire, was ready to defend his crown. In March 1689, a 'packed'
Dublin parliament repealed settlement legislation and passed a bill of
attainder citing over two thousand traitors, including the St Georges,
whose land would enable Ireland's resettlement.[128]

In Leitrim and Roscommon, wealthy Protestants directed by
Robert King of Boyle equipped a militia-style army in support of
King William while Catholics prepared to back King James.[129] In April
1689 the conflict escalated with the Jacobite siege of Derry. Oliver's
eldest son George, having honed his skills in the Great Turkish
War, captained one of four Williamite regiments sent to relieve the
town.[130] Following William's victory at the Battle of the Boyne in
July 1690, the Jacobite army retreated to Connacht where they were
supported by thirteen regiments of local recruits who established a
base at Jamestown.[131] In terms of William's campaign, Carrick fort
offered little strategic advantage, consequently the St George estate
was generally in Jacobite hands and remote from the main action.[132]
Beyond September 1689, the fortress at Carrick disappears from
official record, suggesting that it was decommissioned to guard against
enemy use. Throughout the war, raparees camped in the woods along
the Shannon, benefitting from the covert support of soldiers and
settlers anxious to have a foot in both camps.[133] As the war ended,
skirmishes near Carrick are likely to have provided rich pickings for

the militia who raided livestock to replenish their herds.[134] In October 1691, Limerick, the final Jacobite stronghold, surrendered and the Treaty of Limerick was signed.

The terms of the treaty were generally revoked or ignored and instead of the promised concessions, Catholics were subjected to a series of Penal Laws. Over 14,000 Jacobite soldiers, later known as the 'Wild Geese', were permitted to leave the country. Their departure allowed over one million acres to be confiscated, reducing Catholic landholding to just 14 per cent.[135] In Roscommon 28,933 acres were subject to forfeiture. Despite significant Jacobite loyalty, no land in Leitrim was seized, testimony to the level of dispossession among its Catholic inhabitants.[136] Baronet St George returned to Headford, Co. Galway, the slate wiped clean by the military honour achieved by his eldest son George. Exploiting power and political advantage, the St Georges' combined landholding had increased exponentially. The baronet's greed, extortion and active suppression of Catholics did little to endear him to the native population. Having 'steadily adhered to the king', they resented the benefits reaped by a family of 'Cromwellian tyrants', whose desertion of the 'king's standard' was countered by the timely readjustment of their loyalties.[137] Deprived of land and status, they struggled to come to terms with a treaty the outcome of which constituted what was arguably one of the most serious defeats inflicted on Irish Catholics during the seventeenth century.

2. Paying the price, 1691–1791

Beginning in late seventeenth-century Europe, advances in the fields of science and industry prompted a more reasoned approach to the prospect of social, religious and political change. Throughout most of the eighteenth century, Ireland experienced relative peace. In the context of the negligence displayed by newcomers overcome by land-generated wealth, devotees of improvement focused attention on the duties owed by property owners to those who were property-less.[1] By the mid-eighteenth century, whether driven by economics, religion or guilt-motivated altruism, as observed by Judge Edward Willes, 'a man makes a figure in this country in proportion to the improvements he makes'.[2] Whereas primogeniture was intended to preserve the integrity of an estate, for the St Georges a lack of male heirs led to a disjointed pattern of succession with persons relinquishing possession seeking to extract maximum value from the property while keeping their input to a minimum. In addition, premature death, excessive spending and the cost of socially advantageous marriages all took their toll and the Carrick estate paid the price.

Change was delivered in conjunction with the continued re-engineering of Irish society, the erosion of its culture and the loss of its traditional elite. More than one hundred years after Ireland's eventual conquest, an Irish tract written on behalf of a member of the O'Rourke family bemoaned 'the ignorance of most of the nobility of our land who do not know the things pertaining to their own dignity'.[3] Whereas the writer's concerns highlight the extent to which the descendants of old Irish hierarchies had become part of the new order, the ensuant account of the bravery and betrayal of the O'Rourke chiefs highlights the difficulties associated with integrating the past and the present and the likely impact of those complexities in terms of the shape and momentum of change. The Penal Laws had destroyed the last vestiges of Catholic landownership and ostensibly cemented the power of a predominantly Protestant landed elite. Many Catholics, however, had taken advantage of the growing market economy and successfully engaged in commercial enterprise. A wealthy Catholic merchant class had emerged in the towns and cities with substantial cash assets that, following the passing of the Catholic Relief (Ireland) Act 1782, they were keen to invest in land.[4]

LINEAGE AND THE LAW

The St George family had used power and political advantage to establish a dynasty but its endurance was contingent upon the survival of a legitimate male heir. With biological circumstance interfering with preferred outcomes, creative legal remedies were employed. Baronet Oliver St George died at Headford in 1695, at which point the male line was in jeopardy. In accordance with his last will and testament, his estates were vested in a panel of trustees with a range of family commitments chargeable thereon for a period of seventy years.[5] In 1715, his son George was created Baron St George of Hatley St George in the counties of Roscommon and Leitrim and took his seat in the House of Lords.[6] The family had officially joined the upper echelons of Irish society, reinforcing their roles as prominent members of a 'service nobility' committed to the ministrations of the crown.[7] Lord St George died at Headford in 1735 and was survived by his only child, Mary.[8] In the absence of a direct male heir, the family's brief enrolment to the peerage ended and the estate passed to Richard St George of Kilrush, Co. Kilkenny (fig. 5). Whereas Richard was the legal owner of the property, its use and the distribution of rental income were determined by the earlier trust. Mary's son, George Usher, assumed the St George surname and in 1752 married a wealthy Dublin heiress. As provided for by the 1695 trust, his wife's dowry of £30,000 was secured against the Carrick estate.[9] Usher St George died in January 1775 and his personal fortune was demised to his only surviving child, Emilia.[10] In November 1775, with an income of £4,000 per annum and an estate which was later sold for £60,000, Emilia St George married William FitzGerald, second duke of Leinster.[11] The descendants of Sir George of Carrickdrumrusk had scaled the social ladder and reached the highest ranks of the Irish aristocracy.

Richard St George, great grandnephew of Sir George of Carrickdrumrusk, introduced a new patrilineal line (appendix 2), further complicated the line of descent and compounded the

5. Major General Richard St George, 1744
(Wikipedia, public domain)

family's legal entanglements. A successful career soldier, Richard was appointed lieutenant general of the forces, the most senior military position in Ireland.[12] In 1696, he married Sir George's granddaughter, Elizabeth Coote. Their marriage united the two Irish branches of the St George family but failed to produce a legitimate heir.[13] Richard, however, had two children, Richard and Mary who, as was customary in Ireland, adopted their father's surname.[14] With the help of the attorney general, he secured absolute ownership of his inherited estates enabling him to dispose of the property without restriction.[15] Richard junior purchased a commission in his father's regiment and in 1746, while quartered in Nottingham, is said to have eloped with 16-year-old heiress Mary Blaydwin.[16] The lieutenant general's daughter, 'a lady possessed of the most amiable qualifications, and a considerable fortune', married James Mansergh of Cork.[17] She received a dowry of £6,000, title to the Headford property and £4,000 to be raised on the Carrick estate.[18] Headford Castle became the Mansergh's principal dwelling, their son adopted his mother's surname and the family remained in residence until 1892.[19] The lieutenant general died in 1755, his son Richard received the Carrick estate and a townhouse on Henrietta Street, Dublin. The balance of the estate was shared with his brother-in-law, James Mansergh.[20] Mansergh, however, contested the will and Richard died in 1757, never having benefitted from his inheritance.[21] Ten weeks after his death, his wife gave birth to their only son, who was also called Richard. In 1763, Richard's uncle James obtained a decree for £11,960 to be discharged from the Carrick estate. A loan was raised to clear the debt and an enforced sale was temporarily averted.[22]

Richard St George, who had a propensity for 'young and gay society, ... successive amusements and late hours', did little to improve the fortunes of the Carrick estate.[23] In 1778, at the age of 21, he left Cambridge University, advertised the Carrick estate 'to be let for such terms as shall be agreed' and left Ireland to fight in the American Revolutionary Wars (1775–83).[24] In October 1786, he married Melesina Chenevix, granddaughter of the late bishop of Waterford, 'with a fortune of sixty thousand pounds'.[25] In July 1787 their only surviving child, Charles Manners St George, was born at Henrietta Street. In Carrick, 'bonfires blazed in every quarter of the town' and the tenants' praise of Col. St George's 'content' to allow them 'the means of a comfortable subsistence' barely concealed his lack of involvement in the estate.[26] Despite access to his wife's fortune, Richard had little business acumen and borrowed heavily to support his lifestyle and fulfil the obligations that had been charged against the estate.[27] A bill for foreclosure was filed in December 1789 and St George was served with a decree for £63,845.[28] Three months later Richard died intestate, leaving the entire debt unpaid.[29] His cousin Richard Mansergh St George was similarly prone to excessive spending. Having been injured in America, he left the British Army and spent much of the 1780s on an extended tour of Europe. By the end of the decade, he had depleted his fortune and was forced to return to the Headford estate that he co-owned with his mother Mary.

FROM CARRICKDRUMRUSK TO CARRICK-ON-SHANNON

The complicated interrelationship between title and vested interest prevents the specific input of individual members of the St George family from being accurately interpreted. George and Margaret St George maintained a house in Carrick at least until 1706 but by 1713 they had moved to Headford.[30] Following their marriage in 1714, Mary and John Usher lived intermittently on the Carrick estate but are likely to have moved permanently to Galway *c.*1735, when John succeeded his father-in-law as vice-admiral of Connacht.[31] George Usher St George was nominally associated with Carrick but, apart from the negotiation of leases, appears to have had little involvement with the estate. Following their marriage in 1786, Richard and Melesina St George lived in Co. Meath at Dangan Castle, the seat of the earl of Mornington because, as recorded by Melesina in her diaries, 'neither Mr St George nor his father had ever lived on the family estate' and had no country residence fit for occupation.[32] By comparison, the Kings of Boyle had built Kingston Hall, 'a magnificent and beautiful edifice with extensive and delightful parks' adjoining the rundown manor of Carrickdrumrusk.[33]

By 1700 the fortress at Carrick had been recommissioned, coinciding with billeting restrictions in Britain and the stationing of over 12,000 troops throughout Ireland.[34] In addition to the economic benefits associated with the military influx, access to the town was enhanced by a network of roads connecting the surrounding garrisons. Forced to attend to the neglected needs of the Protestant community, 'a convenient place' in the town was provided for the construction of a parish church.[35] Leases from the early 1700s record the modern anglicized form of Carrickdrumrusk, which appears as 'Carrick-on-Shannon'.[36] By 1714, Leitrim had two boroughs and eighteen villages or gentlemen's seats but, despite the granting of sixteen licences, Carrick was one of only five market-towns to survive.[37] Roscommon

had forty-one villages, but it too had only five market-towns and
relied heavily on Carrick. In 1718, the bridge was replaced by an
eleven-arched structure which improved the socio-economic stature
of the town and marked its emergence as the principal town of the
region.

In 1728 Lord St George secured legal advice relative to the
nature and extent of leases which could be made by parties to the
1695 trust.[38] The opinion addressed the possibility of issuing a
'papist lease' for periods exceeding thirty-one years. Whereas such
leases were considered unsafe, it was explained that irrespective of
religion, leases could not be granted beyond the term of the trust
or the lifetime of the grantor. Consequently, the legal chicanery
occasioned by the circumvention of primogeniture created a situation
whereby the security of tenure offered to Protestant tenants was less
advantageous than might have been achieved elsewhere. Perhaps
evidencing the tenurial circumstance that may have triggered the
need for such advice, six native tenants had secured leases beyond
the permitted thirty-one years. These leases suggest the possibility
of nominal religious conformities or a deliberate attempt to facilitate
the avoidance of penal restrictions through the medium of joint
tenancies. Their execution, combined with the need to seek legal
counsel, demonstrates the disparate attitudes and motivations of the
various parties to the trust and the manifestations of those differences
in terms of leases issued or withheld.

A summary of the 1723 rentals, produced in conjunction with the
case, allows tenurial arrangements to be considered and a picture of
Carrick town and estate to be elicited (appendix 4).[39] Rental income
had increased to £1,095 1s. 16d. compared to £844 9s. 6d. charged in
1681. The number of houses in the town had increased to twenty-
two, as opposed to the earlier figure of just fourteen. Based on the
surnames recorded, Carrick remained a predominantly Protestant
town (table 2). Its planned expansion is implied by the construction
of eight houses, each with a small park, lining the Dublin Road.
The new house plots occupied an area known as 'The Twelve Acres'
which, under the direction of the corporation, had originally been
divided into agricultural parcels linked to specific tenements in the
town.[40] With the increased wealth of the townspeople creating a
demand for higher-quality housing, the redesignation of the town

Table 2. Tenants of Carrick town, 1723

Situation	Tenant	Lease Terms	£	s.	d.
Carrick Town	Anne Tweedy (1)	3 lives	8	18	0
Carrick Town	Anne Tweedy (2)	3 lives	6	6	0
Carrick Town	Bryan Cahan	at will	1	1	0
Carrick Town	Luke Cahan	at will	3	13	6
Carrick Town	John Whittham	3 lives	2	12	6
Carrick Town	Richard Stephens	3 lives	3	13	10
Carrick Town	Matt Sanders	3 lives	3	13	10
Carrick Town	Thomas Griffith (inc. lands Drummagh)	3 lives	11	11	11
Carrick Town	Dominick Maley	at will	2	2	0
Carrick Town	William Constable	at will	2	12	0
Carrick Town	Joseph Whitterass	at will	2	12	0
Carrick Town	Matthew Primrose	at will	6	11	0
Carrick Town	Patrick Sullivan	at will	2	2	0
Carrick Town	Peter Church	3 lives	5	15	6
Carrick Town	Edward Leneghan	21 years	2	12	6
Carrick Town	James Wall	at will	1	11	6
Carrick Town	John Barns	at will	4	4	0
Carrick Town	Charles Davis	at will	3	13	6
Carrick Town	Widow Pritchard	at will	1	11	10
Carrick Town	William White	at will	2	4	0
Carrick Town	Roger Comb	at will	1	1	0
Carrick Town	William Noble	3 lives	2	2	0
The 12 Acres	John Wilson	at will	7	7	0
The 12 Acres	John Wilson (old house)	at will	2	2	0
The 12 Acres	Widow Clifford	3 lives	10	10	0
The 12 Acres	Thomas Hugheston	at will	3	3	0
The 12 Acres	William Little	3 lives	11	11	0
The 12 Acres	Richard Higginson	at will	7	7	0
The 12 Acres	Dick Lloyd	at will	6	6	0
The 12 Acres	Revd Michael Holagon	21 years	3	10	0
Cortubber	Samuel Delashire	at will	21	5	0
Cortubber	Charles Harrison Servant	3 lives	2	12	6
Cortubber	John Gallagher	3 lives	5	5	0
Cortubber	Keilry O'Hara	21 years	9	1	0
Cortubber	Edward Jones	3 lives	5	5	0

(source: St George v. St George (NLI, p4406))

fields positively impacted rental returns and made sound economic sense. On the Roscommon side of the river, five larger houses – some with extensive grounds overlooking the Shannon – brought the number of properties within the greater town area to thirty-five.

Beyond the town, the estate was divided into fifty-five rentals with leases issued in respect of thirty-five tenancies as opposed to twelve in 1681. Twenty-four leases were negotiated for the duration of three specified lives, with the remaining ten properties held by the lessees for a period of twenty-one years. Whereas Protestant settlers held 65 per cent of rural leases, across all religious persuasions 43 per cent of leases were subject to annual negotiation. The frequency of such arrangements may suggest a shortage of suitable tenants or the failure of prospective tenants to commit. It is also possible that some tenants at will availed of low rent-short lease incentives, contingent upon their building a house to an agreed standard. Using leases as an instrument of improvement, tenants were required to plant trees and enclose their lands with walls or double-hedged ditches.[41] Protestant leaseholders were obliged 'to do suite' at the manor court and service the demesne farm.[42] The St Georges retained possession of what has been tentatively identified as the demesne lands at Corsparrow. The original manor house was occupied by Revd William Howard but from 1729 onwards it was leased to successive generations of the Gallagher family, who managed the Carrick estate.[43] In what appears to have been a deliberate attempt to promote the more fertile portion of the estate, a lodge and deer park were constructed on the Roscommon side of the river, switching the demesne focus to a new location contiguous with the estate's corn mills.[44] Notwithstanding the uncertainties that had accompanied the accession of James II, of the five settler families that had held leases in 1681, three remained. Having chosen to advance their prospects in Ireland, they had set down roots on the Carrick estate and were socially and financially committed to a place they had come to regard as their home.

The 1723 rental summaries provide an overview of the estate framework but fail to account for the sub-tenants, cottiers and labourers who constituted the larger portion of its population. Commissioned by the Church of Ireland bishop, Edward Synge, the 1749 'census' of Elphin allows this deficit to be addressed for identifiable townlands in Co. Roscommon (appendix 4).[45] In 1749, there were approximately 1,070 inhabitants, 80 per cent of whom were Catholic, occupying thirty-four townlands in the Elphin diocese that were substantially in the St George's possession. A small number of tailors, glovers, hatters and weavers suggest some localized investment in the textile industry with the names of the tradespersons indicating the introduction of settlers with specific areas of expertise. Throughout the estate, smiths, butchers, coopers, joiners, glazers, shoemakers, merchants, a doctor and an apothecary attest to a basic socio-economic infrastructure supporting an established agricultural community. Sixty-five persons described as 'farmers' represent the lessees or substantial under-tenants who formed the backbone of the estate. There were thirty-seven Protestant families, most of whom were of non-native origin. Evidencing the stratification of settler society, families like the Lawders and Staffords had assumed the status of 'gent', while others like the Roycrofts, Gilmers and Rutledges had furthered their standing in the community by the acquisition of additional holdings, farmed by successive generations. Native Irish surnames of north Roscommon origin, including O'Beirne, Lavin, Leneghan and McDermott, appeared most frequently but the wide range of surnames suggests the continued presence of families forced to relocate during the Cromwellian regime. Conversions to Protestantism were infrequent and occurred mainly in professions from which Catholics were excluded. Mixed marriages were relatively common, the female parties were generally Catholic and children usually followed their mother's faith. In 1749, the townland with the highest Protestant population was Clogher, where James Lawder was the principal tenant. A school had been established in the townland, the proselytizing impact of which is evidenced by a cluster of Protestant children born to Catholic parents.

In 1768, as the descendants of Lieut. General St George struggled with mounting debts, the estate was surveyed and assessed to maximize its economic potential.[46] The total mapped area amounted to 9,153 acres, representing an increase of around 2,500 acres when compared with the documented acreage *c.*1666. Notwithstanding the inclusion of parts of the Shannon, lakes and associated waterways, the increased acreage supports the St Georges' continued acquisition of land during the intervening years. A similar survey of the Headford estate was commissioned by Richard Mansergh St George in 1775.

Whereas both surveys were completed by renowned cartographer Charles Frizell, the Headford survey contained a greater level of detail and appeared not to shy from the more negative aspects of the estate's management.[47] Reflecting the increased demand for land occasioned by the rising population, the presumptive rent chargeable in respect of the Carrick estate was set at £8,183 19s. 3d. per annum. No reference was made to any arrears that may have accumulated or the ability of the tenants to meet their commitments. By comparison at Headford, Frizell claimed to be 'at a loss to know how the tenants ... can propose to themselves paying the presumptive rent nay less the old reserved rent without putting their lands immediately under a proper course of improvement'.[48] There the rent on 4,973 acres was set at £3,413 14s. 1d. annually. At Carrick the number of agricultural plots had increased to ninety-seven compared to fifty-five in 1723. This change in the estate's configuration reflects the redivision of traditional units that had been consolidated when demand for land was low along with the continued subdivision of holdings as the pressure for land increased. Marking the dramatic change in the political landscape, Inishmucker was described as seven acres of good meadow and no longer considered in terms of its military potential. Flax fields, and a bleach yard and bleach mill suggest improvements and diversifications indicative of landlord involvement. The surveyor, however, observed that textile-related enterprises 'might be carried on with great success if properly encouraged', suggesting that such industries were either poorly managed or had ceased to operate. The 'goodness of the land and the beauty of the river' were praised, but unoccupied properties and dilapidated farms evidenced the deterioration of the estate. Further attesting to the lack of landlord engagement, the lodge and demesne in Roscommon were described as 'greatly out of repair'.

Despite the St Georges' limited involvement in the running of the estate, it provided a livelihood for the increasing number of inhabitants who farmed it and may have benefited from the freedom entailed by a landlord's absence. In 1761, on crossing the Shannon at Carrick, Judge Willes noted a 'large field of wheat, the largest I have seen in Ireland'.[49] Having made enquiries in the town, he established that the field, which extended to seventy acres, was cultivated by a group of non-occupant farmers. They paid half of the crop harvested to the holders of adjoining plots, who had chosen to amalgamate part of their holdings. The balance of the crop was said to be divided among the farmers 'for their trouble', enabling them to avail of mutually beneficial economies of scale and secure an income when land was scarce and rents were high.[50] This interpretation of what appears to have been an innovative farming practice compared starkly with the 'oppressive' land usage observed by Richard Mansergh St George at Headford in 1790. There, during the family's protracted absence, the agent was said to have received bribes for the apportionment of a considerable part of the estate to 'land jobbers', who were individually charged rents of up to £1,000 per year. They then 'parcelled out' their holdings to 'sets of eight or ten or more persons' who repeated the process until there were frequently up to five layers of middlemen profiting from the efforts of the eventual occupier.[51] Persons at the bottom of the pyramid struggled to meet their commitments, impacting the layers of payment. By 1790, Mansergh St George alleged that the unpaid arrears of 'land jobbers' had cost the family in the region of £20,000; the 'land was eaten to the bone' and undertenants 'huddled together in huts not habitable by swine'.[52]

Whereas Judge Willes recognized Carrick as the capital of Co. Leitrim and conceded that the town was 'pretty large', he described it as a 'paltry place' that 'afforded nothing worth sending an account of'.[53] The town was serviced by a single water pump, which on the day of the judge's visit was 'out of order', forcing him to drink the 'very bad' water of the Shannon.[54] Produced as part of the 1768 survey, a sketch map of Carrick town provides the earliest representation of the streetscape and supports Willes's observations (fig. 6). The irregular street plan was a product of the original settlement axis of Bridge Street, which extended upwards from the castle and the right-angled development of modern-day Main Street linking the courthouse to the barracks and a second housing cluster, 200m downriver. Apart from a new courthouse, the town showed little evidence of recent landlord involvement. Several residential plots were vacant and a site set aside for a schoolhouse was noted as 'waste'. Despite any significant amenities, the town had continued to grow and contained a total of sixty-five dwellings. Signalling a demographic shift in the estate's urban tenantry, however, more than half of the houses were described

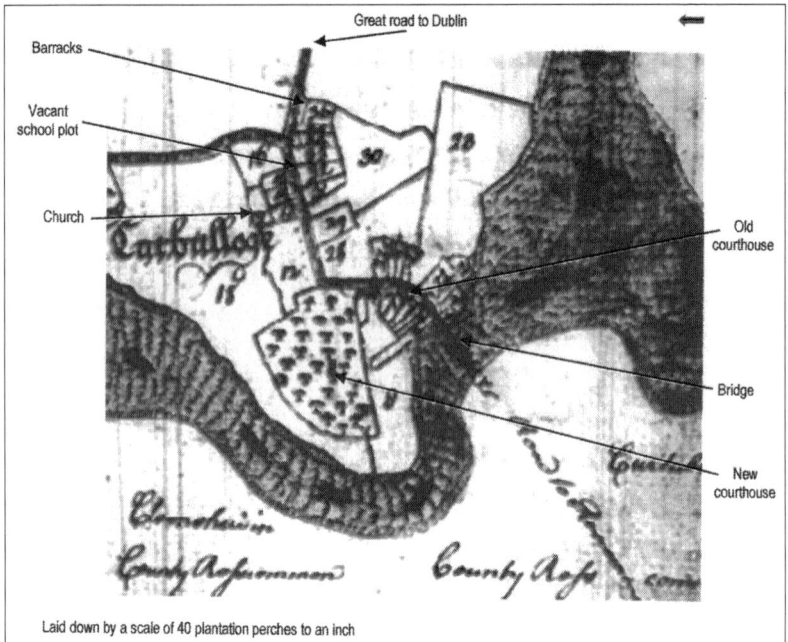

6. Carrick town, 1768 (microfilm p2713)
(reproduced courtesy of the National Library of Ireland)

as 'cabins' and several business proprietors had opted to occupy larger residences on the outskirts of the town. Notwithstanding the lack of recent input attributable to the St Georges, Carrick had achieved shire-town status, surpassing its rival Jamestown.[55] Headford benefited from its proximity to Galway town, but its location relative to the provincial capital limited its administrative potential. In 1775, petty sessions hearings were no longer held in the town and by 1790 the troop had been removed from the barracks.[56] The petty sessions court was subsequently reactivated but, despite a vigorous campaign fought by Mansergh St George, the barracks was not restored.

For much of the eighteenth century, the Carrick estate provided a steady source of income and served as an interim residence for members of the St George family waiting to relocate to Headford. On expiry of the 1695 trust, Headford was vested solely in the descendants of Mary St George Mansergh and was no longer subsidized by Carrick. The St Georges generally failed to deliver or retain the improvements associated with the era and both estates slipped into decline. Emilia St George's inheritance most likely saved the duke of Leinster from bankruptcy, but a similar fortune introduced by Melesina Chenevix was outweighed by apathy, extravagance and the cost of socially beneficial marriages that failed to further the dynasty.[57]

SOLD TO THE HIGHEST BIDDER

In September 1790, pursuant to a decree issued by the court of exchequer, notice was given of the proposed sale of the manor of Carrickdrumrusk 'or a competent part thereof'.[58] On 17 November 1790 the estate was placed under the hammer, to be disposed of in multiple lots to the highest bidders. The public cant was conducted by the chief remembrance officer at his premises at the King's Inns, Dublin.[59] The sale was well attended, with the diverse backgrounds of the perspective purchasers reflecting the cautious sense of national unity that had begun to permeate the political discourse. Below the surface, however, old prejudices and personal grievances simmered. Contributing to the complex nuanced relationships that influenced proceedings, the plaintiff, Henry Bruen of Boyle, was a former army quartermaster, who had reputedly made a fortune through the questionable performance of his duties while on active service in America.[60] In 1783 he assumed the consolidated loans of his much-applauded fellow officer, Richard St George, who pledged the Carrick estate as a security.[61]

Bidding appears to have been strong on the day and sales exceeding £58,600 were achieved. The principal bidder was John Keogh, a Catholic silk merchant of Mount Jerome, Dublin. Keogh bid £16,838 for over 800 acres of prime Roscommon land, which included the ruinous St George lodge and the deer parks at Mullaghatige.[62] John McLoughlin, a merchant with an address at Ushers's Quay, Dublin, purchased lands near the town and a further five lots along the main route to Boyle.[63] In addition, through the agency of Gilbert Roycroft, he acquired an extensive farm occupied by Roycroft, bringing his total outlay to £9,630.[64] Bidding anonymously, Carrick merchant Hugh O'Beirne successfully secured lands around Jamestown together with other miscellaneous lots.[65] O'Beirne had amassed a considerable fortune and in 1785 was residing at Hatley Manor.[66] By the early 1790s, he had leased the town and lands of Jamestown from the Coote family, built an impressive mansion within the town walls and purchased an estate which, at its peak, exceeded 8,000 acres.[67] Further purchases by John Farrell of Bloomfield, Edward Kelly of Kiltoon and Luke Kilmartin of Aghanagilta brought the amount paid by Catholic purchasers to £33,028, over 56 per cent of the total monies expended.[68] The third highest bidder was Robert French, the fifth son of Arthur French of French Park, Co. Roscommon, who was MP for the county and a committed supporter of Catholic relief.[69] Peter La Touche, a Dublin banker and pro-Catholic MP for Co. Leitrim (1783–90), paid £2,200 for lands in Leitrim and Roscommon including the once strategically positioned island of Inishmucker.[70] Various members of the King family, Thomas Lloyd of Athlone, Roscommon merchant Robert Guff, Reynolds Peyton of Castlecarrow, Co. Leitrim, and Sligo landowners Robert Duke and William Phibbs, all made substantial purchases with most Protestant bidders conducting business through their legal representatives.[71]

Highlighting the evolving diversity of Irish landownership, the purchasers included ancient Gaelic families, many with deep-rooted connections to the area, 'old' and 'new' English landowners, and prosperous members of the fluctuating squirearchy. Most were speculators or politicians, intent on expanding their intercounty estates or furthering their political interests. In 1792 it was reported that John Keogh had 'much influence' in Co. Roscommon where he was said to be in receipt of an annual income exceeding £2,000.[72] Farmer Luke Kilmartin was the only leaseholder to successfully bid for the farmstead he worked and occupied. Longstanding Protestant tenants failed to purchase their holdings, with many, like Gilbert Roycroft, renegotiating leasehold arrangements in an environment in which the religiously determined power dynamic was slowly being turned on its head. The enforced sale of the St George estate reconfigured landownership around Carrick, setting the stage for the next phase in the region's tumultuous history. The introduction of new players and the transfer of land to Catholic ownership increased Catholic assertiveness and contributed to the growing apprehension experienced by the Protestant community. The estate had been reduced by over 7,000 acres and responsibility for its survival rested on the shoulders of a 4-year-old boy.

3. The rise of the Catholic community, 1791–1830

In 1803, 16-year-old Charles Manners St George joined the British army and served as *aide de camp* to his guardian, Col. John Craddock. He subsequently graduated from Trinity College, Cambridge, joined the diplomatic service and from 1813 to 1832 held various postings around Europe.[1] In November 1827, at the British Chapel, Genoa, he married Ingri Christina Hallberg of Stockholm.[2] Throughout his nineteen years with the Foreign Office, St George had little direct involvement in the running of his Carrick estate, which from 1814 was managed by non-resident agents Revd William Bermingham and Revd Richard Bermingham. St George's absence, the determination of a small group of Catholic townspeople and a well-educated eloquent clergy, saw Carrick progress from a largely Protestant bastion to a melting pot of religious and political opinions, delivered with equal force by the opposing sides. Bridging the religious dichotomy, an uncertain middle ground represented a less contentious option for socially minded pragmatists whose advancement was inextricably linked to the development of the estate and its community. Given the rapidly evolving political landscape, change was inevitable, but in the absence of whatever overriding authority St George might have exerted, the rate of change generally exceeded the ability of the players to keep pace.

RELIEF AND ITS CONSEQUENCES

In May 1792 the Catholic Committee, which had championed the campaign for civil and political equality since 1757, summoned a thirty-two-county representative convention, which was held at the Tailors' Hall, Dublin. The convention was organized by John Keogh of Mount Jerome, a leading member of the committee. The Leitrim and Roscommon delegates included Keogh, Hugh O'Beirne, John Farrell and John McLoughlin.[3] All four had been successful bidders at the St George estate auction, allowing them to reinforce their status, cement their regional associations and promote their political agendas. Following the convention, Keogh was the acknowledged leader of a five-man deposition whose successful lobbying of King George resulted in the passing of the 1793 Catholic Relief Act.[4] The act allowed Catholics to serve on juries, become members of local corporations and hold commissions in the army. It also extended the franchise to include Catholics in possession of a 40s. freehold. The same year, the Unlawful Assemblies Act effectively silenced the collective voice of the repeal movement while a revised Militia Act disbanded all unregulated volunteer groups and provided for a government-controlled paid militia.[5] The new militia was to be made up of thirty-eight regiments, none of which was to be stationed in their home county. Any shortfall in recruitment was to be addressed by a form of conscription determined by a parochial ballot.

Faced with the threat of conscription and relocation, angry crowds gathered on the streets of Carrick. Members of the lower social orders found a voice through their association with the illegal Defender movement and the gaol was said to be overflowing.[6] In May 1793 St George's guardian, John Craddock, reported that 'the whole of Roscommon and a great part of Sligo and Leitrim were in avowed insurrection'.[7] Despite Catholics having been granted access to local government, their entry was generally contested, allowing judicial remedies to be vigorously enforced by a panic-stricken Protestant gentry. With public executions and floggings acting as a deterrent, Defenderism waned and a brief period of calm was restored. In August 1794, Carrick's influential inhabitants agreed to mutually forgive all past injuries and 'act in concert and friendship … for the detection and apprehension of all Defenders or takers of unlawful oaths'.[8] The 1793 Relief Act, however, had done little to address the hardships endured by the less well-off. Poorer Catholics were becoming increasingly aggrieved by the extent of church tithes, fees paid to Catholic priests and the perceived lack of support shown by their wealthy brethren. By March 1795 it was reported that around Carrick, Defenders were marching at night to the clamour of fife and drum, administering unlawful oaths, committing outrages and instilling fear in the community.[9] While those with a vested interest in maintaining peace pledged their solidarity, small farmers struggled to maintain a living, discontent festered and Defenderism again gained momentum. A Defender catechism, found in the pocket of a man executed at Carrick gaol, cited the organization's pledge to 'dethrone all kings and to plant the true religion that was lost at the reformation'.[10] Whereas Defenderism was underpinned by anti-state and anti-Protestant ideologies, its broad principles supported the annexing of an array of local grievances which facilitated the organization's expansion. Notices posted on chapel doors in Leitrim not only ordered the non-payment of tithes to the Established Church but also demanded the lowering of fees collected by the Catholic clergy.[11] As the Defenders scrambled to equip their predominantly Catholic numbers, it was alleged that all Protestants within a forty-mile radius of Carrick had been forcibly divested of their arms.[12] The disquiet was compounded by rumours of a French invasion reputedly pursued by newcomer John Keogh and his *protégé* Theobald Wolfe Tone (1763–98).

Illicit distilling was rampant and unlicensed whiskey outlets were regarded by the forces of law and order as a breeding ground for Defenders.[13] In April 1795, six miles (9.5km) from Carrick, revenue officers, having been forced to flee from a burning building, were attacked with scythes and pitchforks. The same day, over three thousand Defenders confronted soldiers of the Derry militia at the nearby village of Drumsna.[14] Large numbers of troops were redeployed to the county and it was reported that 'from the great quantity of blood on the roads … it is impossible to form an idea of the vast numbers that are killed and wounded'.[15] As the 'lower orders' around Carrick continued to be in a 'state of great inquietude and fermentation', the situation was exacerbated by the arrival of large numbers of Catholic weavers fleeing from Armagh.[16] Faced with the threat of hell or Connacht, they escaped the wrath of the Loyal Orange Order and, like the seventeenth-century Ulster Creaghts, took refuge in Leitrim or trudged across the county which was once again a gateway to the west.[17] The northern refugees fanned the flames of rebellion and enabled the newly formed United Irishmen (1791–1804) to gain a foothold in the county. By the summer of 1798, having endured five years of mutually inflicted brutality, the Catholic and Protestant inhabitants of Carrick co-existed in an environment sustained by fear and necessity. With the main protagonists executed, incarcerated or fearing for their lives, United Irish numbers fell significantly. During the summer of 1798, as risings took place throughout Ireland, Leitrim remained poised on the periphery but the repercussions of earlier insurrections had taken their toll. For the inhabitants of the St George estate, the rebellion had already occurred.

On 22 August 1798 General Humbert and just over one thousand French troops sailed into Killala Bay.[18] With an extensive military campaign underway, Carrick's strategic location once again impacted its fate. The lord lieutenant, Charles Cornwallis, first Marquess Cornwallis (1738–1805), pledged to march immediately to Carrick and command proceedings in person.[19] Over the next weeks Humbert and Cornwallis played cat and mouse across Connacht with the lord lieutenant in command of 'a superior force of 30,000 troops'.[20] British officers reported that the country continued to be disposed in their favour, but conceded that this was not 'absolutely the case towards Carrick'.[21] The Leitrim militia was deployed to Rathdrum, Co. Wicklow, and the city of Limerick militia assisted the military at Carrick. The French falsely leaked their intention to ford the Shannon at Carrick causing Cornwallis to rush to the town only to find 'that the enemy had passed the Shannon at Ballintra'.[22] Having marched for eighteen days Hubert reached Ballinamuck, Co. Longford, where, with his men tired, hungry and hopelessly outnumbered, he surrendered. Rank-and-file soldiers were brought to Carrick, before being dispatched to Dublin *en route* to France.[23] One-hundred-and-thirteen rebels were conveyed to Carrick courthouse where, on receipt of orders from Cornwallis, seventeen men were chosen by lots and 'as fast as a wretch drew the fatal ticket he was handed out and hanged at the door'.[24] The military converged on the route travelled by the French, rooting out suspects and carrying out executions and punishments with a level of brutality that was more about subjugation than justice. Whereas Carrick was not within the target zone, as a county and sessional town its inhabitants witnessed, or were party to, the excessive remedies authorized by agents of the crown. At the height of the harvest season, its agricultural hinterland was trampled upon by a massive army the magnitude of which had never been seen in the region. In time-honoured tradition, the inhabitants of Leitrim were among the 'first out in action', but the repercussions of their premature endeavours meant that, on this occasion, they were not among the last to submit.[25]

Ireland had experienced its first major uprising in over one hundred years. The merchant community generally bounced back, but small farmers lost their livelihoods and in the winter of 1798 were in a state of near starvation. John Keogh was reputed to have used his personal fortune to further the rebellion. Consequently, in an ironic turn of events, rents received from former parts of the St George estate may have indirectly subsidized the war. Constrained by timing and the premature deaths of successive male heirs, for the first time in their long association with Ireland, the St Georges of Carrick failed to reap the benefits of military advantage. Far-removed from the trauma, Charles was too young to have any understanding of these events. His father's cousin, Richard Mansergh St George, travelled to Cork to quell unrest on his Macrony estate and in February 1798 was murdered by a gang of Defenders, reputedly acting on the orders of the United Irishmen.[26] Further evidencing the St Georges' continued allegiance to the crown, Charles's guardian, Col. Craddock, saw active service in 1798 and was wounded by French troops near the Co. Leitrim village of Cloone.[27] Throughout this period of unrest, Charles's mother travelled extensively in Germany, where her lifestyle contrasted starkly with the conditions endured on her son's estate. Her diverse group of acquaintances included British princes Henry and Adolphus, the duke of Wellington and Admiral Nelson. While in Hamburg, she met the exiled and recently widowed Lady Edward FitzGerald. Despite FitzGerald's husband having been one of the principal agents of the rebellion, Melesina made no reference to the circumstance of his death. She was, however, enthralled by his little daughter, whose eyelashes she described as 'celestial'.[28]

UNION, DISUNION AND CONTINUED DISTRESS

The 1798 Rebellion highlighted the extent of Ireland's political volatility and Britain's urgent need to bring matters under control. Duke Crofton esq., one of Leitrim's few resident landlords, maintained that a union with Britain was the only way of 'preventing Roman Catholics from stealing into parliament'.[29] Myles Keon, who had been at the forefront of the repeal movement, also welcomed a union, but believed that it represented Ireland's best chance of achieving full emancipation. In Leitrim 1,386 Catholic freeholders registered their support for a union and a further 1,500 signatures were secured in Roscommon.[30] Notwithstanding the extent of pro-union support, the anti-union movement also had a considerable following. Signalling the power of anti-union exponents, Keon insisted that 'none but the signatures of noblemen and gentlemen of known property and freehold should be published at full length'.[31] Whereas small farmers had been granted a voice and had indicated their political opinion, they lacked the protection afforded by wealth and status and were forced to resort to collective anonymity.

In January 1801 the Act of Union was passed and Ireland became part of the United Kingdom of Great Britain and Ireland. The inhabitants of the St George estate waited for the dust to settle. In 1806, anxious to dissociate themselves from the rebellion, the Catholics of Leitrim gathered at Carrick courthouse and in anticipation of 'continued wise and liberal policy' pledged their support to the empire.[32] The meeting was chaired by Hugh O'Beirne of Jamestown, who was fast becoming one of Leitrim's most important inhabitants. Having ensured that his two sons, both lawyers, had been given 'the best education' he could afford, O'Beirne used his influence to secure the support of the earls of Leitrim, making 'friends' for his sons, which he trusted they 'would have the judgment to keep'.[33] While the upper echelons of Carrick society protected their interests and debated the political consequences, the small farmers and labourers, who constituted the greater proportion of the estate's population, struggled to survive. By 1817, the union's promised concessions had not materialized and tensions had begun to mount. In the context of increasing opposition, a group of predominantly Protestant freeholders assembled in Carrick and made clear their determination to 'resist every attempt that may be made' to subvert the constitution.[34] Whereas the broadening of the franchise enabled Carrick's wealthy Catholics to secure a pro-Catholic voice, for many 40s. freeholders the vote was a double-edged sword. Small farmers, who made up the greater part of the electorate, were considered 'too poor to have political interest', but their votes were a valuable commodity.[35] The parliamentary borough of Carrick was abolished in 1801 and the number of representatives returned by the county was reduced to two. From 1805 to 1818, Col. Henry John Clements of Ashfield Lodge, Co. Cavan, held one of the two county seats. A strong Tory and opponent of Catholic relief, it was alleged that he threatened freeholders who voted against him, filling the pounds around Carrick with their livestock and driving them 'to beggary by vexation and persecution'.[36] The O'Beirnes, having aligned themselves with the Clements family, backed the pro-Catholic Whig candidate introduced by Lord Leitrim. They actively canvassed the Carrick electorate, leaving St George's tenants to choose between two undesirable alternatives.

Britain's victory at Waterloo reduced the demand for Irish agricultural produce. The situation was exacerbated by bad weather, poor harvests and increasing unrest, triggering a period of severe economic distress. Highlighting the extent of the problem, Hugh O'Beirne's younger son Francis explained how 'everything termed property has been gradually sacrificed to the demands of the tithe proctor, the collector of county cess, and the needy impoverished landlord'.[37] Weakened by poverty and despair, the poorer classes were increasingly susceptible to disease. Between June 1817 and March 1819, more than 20 per cent of the population of Carrick town contracted typhoid fever. In its immediate vicinity, a further 256 residents became ill, bringing the total number infected to 558 persons.[38] At the height of the epidemic, St George donated a townhouse on Gallows Hill for use as a county infirmary. The old infirmary plot was leased to Carrick architect, Robert Robinson, for £11 1s. 6d. annually.[39] By mid-1819, fever levels had been brought under control, but with low wages, unemployment and rising prices the economy continued to deteriorate and the county was reduced to a state of crisis.

In May 1822 the London Tavern Committee was established to alleviate distress in Ireland. Faced with impending disaster, the gentlemen of Leitrim and Roscommon bombarded the Committee with 'very urgent solicitations' and secured a promise of partial relief.[40] As the cost of potatoes rose from 5d. to 4s. per cwt, the poor around Carrick were said to be surviving on 'the tops of wild turnips, spinach and watercress'.[41] The 'principal inhabitants' of the parish of Kiltoghert met at Carrick courthouse and pledged their support. Two weeks later, they acknowledged receipt of £100 in government funds and a further £185 9s. 6d. raised by public subscription.[42] It was resolved that of the 15,097 inhabitants of Kiltoghert parish (approximately 3,019 families), only 874 families had sufficient income to buy oats at the reduced price funded by the committee. A further 573 families were found to be 'altogether destitute' and this number was said to be increasing daily. Thirty-six subscribers contributed to the initial fund, including the parish priest, Revd John McKeon, whose donation of £2 5s. 6d. most likely represented the proceeds of a church collection. He subsequently raised £17 from a charity sermon preached in the town.[43] Francis O'Beirne contributed £25 and, along with other gentlemen of the district, established boilers for the free distribution of soup.[44] St George donated £10 and the proceeds of materials salvaged during demolition of the old courthouse. The vacant site was later leased to aspiring property developer Captain Charles Cox of the Leitrim militia.[45] At Headford, Richard Mansergh St George junior described a similar level of poverty but in addition to subscribing to the local relief fund, he claimed to have supported 111 families at his expense.[46]

In July 1822, the Co. Leitrim Central Committee was established and the management of distress was placed on a formal footing. Francis O'Beirne was elected chairman and Catholic militia officer, George McDermott of Carrick, was pronounced secretary and treasurer.[47] By August, 12,607 households were in receipt of relief, of which 2,076 were in the parish of Kiltoghert.[48] Whereas the Leitrim committee was commended for the 'business-like manner' in which the fund had been administered, political and religious discord gradually clouded the judgment of its members, inciting sectarian bitterness.[49] In the wake of the crisis, the social and political implications were assessed and old power-based insecurities reared their heads. Francis O'Beirne had undoubtedly been at the forefront of the relief process and filled a role that might otherwise have fallen to a St George. He helped raise the stature of the Catholic landlord but ruffled the feathers of a Protestant squirearchy that, throughout the process, had been loath to either take or relinquish control. In giving thanks to the London Tavern Committee, O'Beirne illustrated Ireland's increasing political assertiveness, pointing out that England had not only received 'reward in the gratitude of Irishmen' but also in 'great political advantage'.[50]

In an official assessment of Ireland's distress, the London Tavern Committee acknowledged absentee landlords as a 'primary evil'.[51] Proprietors who 'take several millions of rent annually out of the country' were called upon to return to their estates or be prepared to forgo a sizeable portion of their rental incomes. In May 1826 St George made a rare visit to his estate and reputedly 'made considerable reductions to his tenantry'.[52] The discount was made in the context of a rental income said to be less than £1,600 per annum.[53] This figure equates to 10s. 8d. per acre, based on the combined commercial and agricultural acreage of the estate. In 1802, reasonably fertile land in Leitrim achieved 20s.–30s. per acre, with agricultural holdings close to Carrick town expected to command more than 40s. per acre.[54] Whereas consideration must be given to the accuracy of the figures quoted, post-war reductions, soil quality and the extent of untenanted lands, the presumed rental income appears less than could have been charged.

THE 'SECOND REFORMATION'

In January 1823 Francis O'Beirne reluctantly acknowledged religious conflict to be 'the great bane of Ireland's prosperity'.[55] In the years that followed, his words were proven to be particularly apt as the inhabitants of Carrick embraced the evangelical ethos of Ireland's so-called 'Second Reformation'. By 1823, with Ireland's great leader Daniel O'Connell (1775–1846) spearheading the crusade for Catholic emancipation, religion and politics dominated all levels society and became mutually endorsing co-dependencies. The Co. Leitrim Auxiliary Bible Society held its 'numerous and highly respectable' inaugural meeting at Carrick courthouse on 24 October 1823. The Protestant gentlemen turned up in force in their first overt display of authority since the 1822 crisis.[56] The meeting was addressed by Robert King, Viscount Lorton of Boyle, a steadfast Conservative and supporter of the Loyal Orange Order. William Irwin, Leitrim's pro-Catholic high sheriff, was unavailable and the chair was taken by Sir Josias Rowley, an unwavering opponent of Catholic relief.

In November 1824 Carrick became the focus of the evangelical movement when the parish priest, Revd McKeon, challenged the

Bible Society to an open debate. The press engaged in an editorial frenzy, which fanned the flames of sectarianism and reputedly reduced the town to a state of 'intense anxiety'.[57] The Protestant clergy, it was claimed, were ready to engage with the politically motivated 'bludgeon' wielding 'Professors of Popery' who in their turn, it was declared, had promised to exercise the real 'spirit of Christian liberality' and their 'profound veneration of the sacred scriptures'.[58] In 1823 Carrick's first free school was established and purportedly adhered to in the non-denominational principles of the Kildare Place Society. St George donated the site and contributed £80, subject to a similar amount being furnished by subscription.[59] The following year, an audit by the society uncovered anti-Catholic tracts, stored in a schoolroom cupboard.[60] As both denominations paraded a constant stream of alleged conversions, and Catholics swelled the ranks of the militia, McKeon abandoned all semblance of 'Christian liberality' and gave vent to his frustration. He directed his wrath at army recruitment parties whom he maintained preyed on 'every barelegged, bog-trotting deserter', bribing them to enlist in the military and then clapping 'the cockade of Protestantism' into their hats.[61] The escalation of religious animosity coincided with St George's 1826 visit, perhaps prompting the inhabitants of Carrick to present a united front and placate McKeon with a dinner in his honour. To great applause, the reverend gentleman raised a glass to the prosperity of the town and the good health of its proprietor. The usual tributes having been made, McKeon wound up proceedings with a carefully worded toast saluting 'civil and religious liberty' and 'union and content to all his majesty's subjects'.[62]

Fuelled by the press and the posturing clergy, religion become a spectator sport with the number of alleged converts dictating the score. Whereas O'Connell had initially viewed the debates as a treat to peace, by 1827 he was chairing a series of high-profile debates at the Dublin Institution where Revd Tom Maguire, parish priest of Innishmagrath, Co. Leitrim, was described as a leading light.[63] Notwithstanding the biased portrayal of sensationalized extremes, religious rivalry created opportunities that might otherwise have been less expediently delivered. By September 1826 seven schools had been established in Carrick with approximately 253 pupils in attendance (table 3). A further seventy-three inmates received educational

Table 3. Carrick schools, 1826

Location	Description	Pay/ Free	Patronage	Scriptures	Name	Religion	Wage/ Income	Prot.	R.C.	M	F
Carrick	Gaol	Free (Gaol)	Kildare Place	Read Irish and English	Michael McDermott	Prot.	£17 10s.	3	70	73	0
Carrick	Room house	Pay	None	Read Greek	Patrick Jas McDonnell	R.C.	£60	8	22	30	0
Carrick	Private room	Free	Kildare Place C.M. St George	Read	James Morriss	R.C.	£3 £20	25	33	52	6
Carrick	Room house	Pay	None	Read	John Logue	R.C.	£35	16	15	19	12
Carrick	Private room	Free	Revd McKeon subscriptions	Not read	Mary Leonard	R.C.	£10	0	20	0	20
Carrick	Loft	Pay	None	Not read	Bartholomew Dunn	R.C.	£61	27	22	33	16
Carrick	Small room	Free	Ladies' Hib. Sch. Soc.	Read	Mary Barlow	Prot.	£16	10	11	0	21
Cortober	Built £10	Pay	None	Read (Prot) Not read (R.C.)	Michael Murray	R.C.	£16	3	41	32	12

(source: *Second report of the commissioners of Irish education inquiry*, pp 1244–5)

instruction in the gaol. Reflecting a level of religious accord which belied the media coverage, schools under the direction of Roman Catholic teaching staff recorded a total Protestant attendance of 34 per cent. The all-girl school sponsored by the Hibernian School Society retained a Protestant schoolmistress who taught a class of twenty-one students in which the religious composition was almost equally proportioned. In accordance with the religiously motivated philanthropy that facilitated the schools' existence, scripture-reading either formed part of or was excluded from the curricula. In some instances, translation of the bible into Irish or Greek disguised a proselytizing agenda or allowed religious connotations to be pragmatically circumvented. Notwithstanding its earlier difficulties, the Kildare Place Society continued to endorse a free school. A

Catholic master had been placed in charge and his wages were paid by
St George. At Headford, the Mansergh St George family contributed
to the wages of the teaching staff employed at the parish school. There
the master, the mistress and all thirty-one students were members of
the Established Church.[64]

In the spirit of diplomatic ecumenism, St George had provided
sites in the town for the construction of Catholic and Protestant
places of worship. At the height of the 'Second Reformation', with
the press eager to entertain their readers, his diplomatic skills were
put to the test. In January 1827 it was reported that St George's agent,
Revd Bermingham, had used excessive force to evict a family whose
temporary accommodation had been demolished to provide access to
the new Protestant church. St George was berated by the press for
the 'shocking barbarity perpetrated in order to beautify the entrance
to the "Law" Church'.[65] Bermingham refuted the allegations and
encouraged the Catholics of Carrick to be mindful of the benefits
that they too had received. He further begged leave to assure the
estate's Roman Catholic tenantry that St George would not be
deterred by this incident and would continue to adhere to 'the same
line of impartial and unprejudiced conduct which he has invariably
followed'.[66]

'STEALING INTO PARLIAMENT'

Barrister O'Connell assumed the baton of Catholic emancipation
with his successful campaign earning him the title 'the Liberator'. He
aimed to achieve full emancipation, through the mass mobilization of
Catholics in a self-supporting non-violent campaign, delivered within
the framework of the Union. This was to be achieved through the
well-orchestrated machinations of the Catholic Association, funded
by a membership subscription of one penny per month. O'Connell's
tactics were successfully put to the test at the 1826 general election.
With the canvassing power of the clergy and the security of the
'Catholic rent', voters, who had previously bowed to pressure or
intimidation, favoured the pro-Catholic candidate. Three nominees
contested the Leitrim seats, Viscount Robert Bermingham Clements,
who had been proposed by Francis O'Beirne, the anti-Catholic

John Marcus Clements and sitting Whig member Samuel White. At the last minute, John Marcus Clements withdrew and White and Viscount Robert Bermingham Clements were returned unopposed. St George's visit to Carrick in 1826, conveniently coinciding with the election, allowed him to declare his support for Viscount Clements and nail his political colours to the pro-Catholic mast.[67]

By January 1828 simultaneous meetings of the Catholic Association had taken place throughout Connacht. The renowned orator Tom Maguire officiated at the association's meeting in Carrick, no arrests were made and the crowd dispersed in an orderly manner. It was reported that whereas 'Catholic rents' had been sporadically collected, the meetings generally 'failed in effect'.[68] The following June, O'Connell contested a by-election in Clare and secured a parliamentary seat on behalf of the association. Faced with what had become a formidable force, Carrick's conservative Protestants closed ranks. In October 1828 supporters of the suppressed Orange Order established the Carrick Brunswick Club with Henry John Clements at the helm.[69] In response, the Friends of Civil and Religious Liberty of the County of Leitrim, a newly established electoral organization, invited their 'much valued Protestant friends' to attend their next meeting and express support for the emancipatory process.[70] At a similar meeting held in Longford the following week, cracks in the Protestant-O'Connellite alliance were exposed. Lord Forbes, one of the county's principal landlords, objected to a proposed vote of thanks to O'Connell and his misgivings were ignored. Like many liberal Protestants forced to acknowledge the erosion of status precipitated by the O'Connell machine, Forbes parted company with his Whig colleagues and realigned with the Tories.[71] The Leitrim 'Friends' met in Carrick on 11 December 1828. Notwithstanding events in Longford, the meeting was chaired by Lord Leitrim, whose support on the platform included his son, Lord Clements, Maguire, McKeon and O'Beirne. The *Roscommon and Leitrim Gazette* openly opposed emancipation and having been formally boycotted by the 'liberals', had an axe to grind. They inferred that most of the attendees were 'landed proprietors' who between them did not own a 'square inch' of land in the county. Lord Leitrim, it was implied, was so out-dazzled by the oratory skills of Maguire that he 'was obliged to put an extinguisher on him'.[72] The writer, however, chose to remain silent regarding the potentially contentious vote of thanks to O'Connell. As the *Gazette* hit the newsstands, the 'Protestants of Carrick' put their best feet forward and petitioned parliament for the suppression of the Catholic Association. They argued that the primary motivation of the organization was to keep the country 'in a state of agitation' until their demands were met.[73] Less than three months later, faced with the power of the Catholic electorate and a defence force that was no longer in the Protestant domain, the final Roman Catholic Relief Act became law.[74]

As had occurred in 1793, concessions afforded by the 1829 Relief Act were countered by changes that impacted the anticipated outcome. By January 1830, with voters required to possess freehold interests worth at least £10, eligibility in Leitrim had fallen to 602 compared with 6,361 the previous year.[75] Reflecting the distribution of wealth in the county, the majority of those disenfranchised were Catholic. In Carrick, local priests appealed to parishioners to assert their independence by supporting a Roman Catholic candidate.[76] In 1831 it was intimated that the pro-reformist Francis O'Beirne intended to run for election but, despite being regarded as a 'formidable opponent', he considered it a step too far and opted instead to serve as high sheriff.[77] Faced with a political dilemma, John Reynolds Peyton eventually accepted the nomination of the anti-reform Tories, alongside John Marcus Clements.[78] Peyton was of Irish and planter stock and in terms of religion had a foot in both camps. He was 'heir-at-law' to the Reynolds of Lough Scur whose ancestors had supported the crown and served as high sheriffs in 1613 and 1621.[79] In offering his candidature, Peyton acknowledged his ascendancy background and, citing 'the dangers of complete alteration and the advantages of beneficial amendment', he advocated a measured approach.[80] Having tested the waters, however, Peyton found 'the great majority of the constituency adverse ... to the principles which he professed' and respectfully withdrew.[81] Contrary to the views expressed by Duke Crofton, the Union had failed to prevent 'Catholics from stealing into parliament' but, centuries of religious and cultural suppression had left their mark. In Leitrim, as in many Irish counties, social realities fell short of the dream and impeded the realization of the long-awaited constitutional right. The Clements and White families continued to retain political dominance and despite high levels of post-Emancipation enthusiasm, Leitrim did not return a Catholic candidate until 1852.

THRESHING IT OUT

In contrast to the peaceful remedies employed by O'Connell and the aspiring middle-class Catholics who hoped to reap the benefits of emancipation, more aggressive tactics were adopted by secret agrarian societies who addressed the perceived injustices associated with tithes and abuses of tenure. The ink was barely dry on the Act of Union when it was reported that large meetings, under the pretence of football games, were taking place at remote chapels throughout Leitrim.[82] Proponents of Defenderism re-emerged as 'Threshers', pledging to 'observe the Thresher laws, to go out when called upon and to pay no tithes except to the Rector'.[83] Amid mounting unrest and charges of magisterial misconduct, indictments at Carrick court remained low and reputedly evinced 'the happy state of tranquillity' enjoyed by the county.[84] Most likely contributing to this 'tranquillity', up to 110 privates and four officers manned the army garrison and until July 1813 a further four officers and 122 men were quartered in temporary accommodation in the town.[85] In 1809 66 per cent of privates recruited to the Leitrim militia were Catholic and in Roscommon the number was almost 88 per cent. The Roscommon militia was controlled by the Kings of Boyle who insisted that all officers were members of the Established Church. By comparison, in Leitrim 'the paymaster, one lieutenant, the surgeon and his mate' were Roman Catholic, reflecting the liberal politics of those influencing appointments.[86] Whereas militia units were not deployed in their county of origin, officers of the Leitrim militia were frequently excused to attend to their civil duties and enjoyed the stature afforded by their rank while generally remaining in their hometown. In August 1822 the Royal Irish Constabulary, Ireland's first countrywide police force, was established.[87] Ninety-six constables were assigned to Co. Leitrim, sixteen in each barony. By 1828, only one corporal and six privates were stationed in Carrick army garrison and responsibility for law and order had largely devolved to the new police force.[88]

In the context of extreme poverty, social upheaval and discontent with the outcome of the Union, the new police force experienced the full gamut of criminal activity. Members of the banned Orange Order resumed their marches, rioting escalated and, with 'alarming and well-armed parties of nightly insurgents', Rockites or Ribbonmen enforced their own version of justice.[89] In March 1828 there were sixteen 'Rockites' and eleven rioters incarcerated in Carrick gaol.[90] Soldiers from the garrison were attacked, witnesses at Carrick court required police protection and informants were promised free passage to America.[91] With Carrick straddling two counties, the asylum offered by 'ill-disposed persons' on the Roscommon side of the river posed a problem for the judicature. It was proposed that the powers of resident Carrick magistrate Captain Charles Cox be extended to address this anomaly.[92] In January 1828, a sixty-yard wall on the St George estate was pulled down and the tenant, Captain Cox, was served with a threatening notice. This attack was specifically directed at Cox who, in addition to his cross-county magisterial functions, had been implicated by Daniel O'Connell in his defence of an assault charge brought against the golden-voiced Maguire.[93]

As the level of unrest increased, the overstretched constabulary refused to assist in the repossession of property or collection of outstanding tithes. In response, it was intimated that if support was not given 'the practice of raising a *posse comitatus*' would present an even greater threat to the county.[94] O'Connell made a specific appeal to the people of Carrick to 'abandon their ribbon societies', but his request was largely ignored.[95] In December 1829 Cox informed the chief secretary that the 'spirit of Whiteboyism ... in this part of Leitrim' was in danger of accelerating out of control.[96]

CARRICK ESTATE AND TOWN

For the first three decades of the Union, few primary sources have survived that relate specifically to the rural portion of the estate. Throughout Co. Leitrim, it was reported that there were no agricultural societies, farming methods were generally primitive, no attempt was made to promote manufacture and access roads were 'shamefully broken and bad'.[97] Gilbert Roycroft, a tenant most likely introduced by the St George family *c.*1713, was one of the few progressive farmers in the region. Producing 'beef and mutton as fat and as nice flavoured as anywhere to be met with', his holding near Carrick was among the first lots to fall under the hammer in 1790.[98]

In the early nineteenth century Carrick town had the basic infrastructure required to support its county and garrison functions. Individual merchants met the needs of their clientele but, in the context of sectarian feuding and an absent proprietor, there was no cohesive plan for its development. The St Georges, having sold the borough in 1757, no longer controlled the council. Following its disenfranchisement, the Clements had little interest in the town and by 1826 the corporation had ceased to exist.[99] As during the preceding century, the town continued to evolve randomly with little organized effort made to improve the living conditions of its inhabitants. In 1801 it was still without a free school or a functioning infirmary, the gaol was overcrowded and its proposed restructure had been accompanied by the doubling of grand-jury cess.[100] In December 1803 the first boats carrying a cargo of potatoes made the journey from Carrick to the Grand Canal Harbour, Dublin.[101] Inadequate docking facilities and excessive lockage duties impacted the commercial viability of the route. Carrick failed at this point to develop as a significant river port and was used almost solely for the transport of military baggage and slates.[102] By 1807 the town was described as being 'principally composed of one straggling street with here and there a tolerable decent house and a multitude of cabins'.[103] The trade of the town was said to be 'scarcely anything' but appeared to be improving.[104] In the wake of the 1798 Rebellion, Carrick's streetscape was dominated by two barracks with capacity for six companies of foot and a new gaol that a writer hoped 'for the sake of humanity [would] never be entirely wanting for the purpose of incarceration'.[105] Outside the gaol 'the drop, the pulleys, the spikes on which to put men's heads' served as a grim reminder to would-be offenders.[106] By 1821 the population of Carrick town had risen to 1,673 persons.[107] The number of inhabited houses had increased to 230 from 65 in 1768. Reflecting the level of poverty, approximately 31 per cent of the town's inhabitants shared their homes with at least one other family. In Headford town a population of 1,228 persons was recorded but, with just 16 per cent living in shared accommodation, the impact of recent improvements was evident.

The 1822 crisis had provoked a period of religiously motivated civic responsibility that operated in tandem with under-funded government interventions driven by the need to maintain control. Carrick town acquired a new infirmary, seven schools, three new churches, a new courthouse, a new gaol and a constabulary barracks. Multiple retailers and service providers also established premises in the town. In many cases, new entrants replaced pre-existing ventures that had fallen foul of the bankruptcy courts. Notwithstanding these improvements, in 1826 Lord Leitrim, having secured the support of the Carrick electorate, voiced his disgust at having been assailed on the road to Mohill by a 'mob of paupers ... vociferating together and crying out for money in the most violent and clamorous manner'.[108] Openly signalling St George's minimal involvement with the estate, Hatley Manor house and demesne was leased to farmer John Houston Bournes, one the estate's principal tenants.[109] By comparison, at Headford, where St George's cousin was said to be in possession of a 'fine demesne, extensively planted from his own designs' it was suggested that 'if every landlord possessed half as much energy and taste ... the county would assume a very different appearance'.[110]

In September 1827 it was rumoured that the Carrick estate was to be sold and Francis O'Beirne was named as a likely purchaser. Evidencing the increased confidence of the Catholic community and an acceptance of the shifting social dynamic, the *Gazette* hailed the change of ownership 'with much satisfaction' and were confident that O'Beirne would lend the 'fostering hand' necessary to enable Carrick to become 'one of the most flourishing towns in the province'.[111]

4. 'It is finished', 1830–64

In 1832 Charles Manners St George (fig. 7) retired from the diplomatic service and returned to Carrick, further complicating the fragile social dynamic to which the community had yet to adjust. He attempted to rescale the social ladder and reaffirm the legacy initiated by Sir George of Carrickdrumrusk. St George's return coincided with the Great Famine, a crisis of unprecedent proportions which would put the estate, its landlord and its people to the test. St George combined political expedience with philanthropic endeavour and, employing every skill in his diplomatic arsenal, attempted to assert control of the dwindling middle ground. Landlord and tenant engaged in a well-orchestrated dance where, with socially hierarchies continually being challenged, St George was about to discover that paying the piper was no longer rewarded with calling the tune.

CALLING THE TUNE

In May 1830 St George and his wife arrived in Carrick. With his resignation from the Foreign Office in the offing, the visit enabled him to assess his options and address expectations in terms of the management of his estate. He assumed the role of a benevolent landlord and, adopting an appropriate level of obsequiousness, his tenants played along. The town was 'brilliantly illuminated' and the couple were 'hailed with every possible demonstration of joy'.[1] The St Georges visited the gaol and paid the debts of several prisoners who were duly released. Harking back to comments made following his visit in 1826, Charles declared his intention to provide the 'fostering hand' necessary to render Carrick 'worthy of being the county town'.[2] He gave directions for the construction of a gallery in the Catholic chapel and a meat-shambles in the centre of the town. With the original manor house occupied by tenants and no country residence at his disposal, St George announced that an architect had been commissioned to execute plans for a new inn. These initial ventures demonstrate the combination of economic pragmatism and carefully measured diplomacy that were to characterize St George's actions in the years to come.

Having moved in diplomatic circles throughout Europe, St George was acutely aware of the rapidly changing socio-political landscape and, like his military forbears, was aptly positioned to follow a course of action determined by the 'the political wind'.[3] He supported a version of nationalism that allowed him to maintain favour with the county's Protestant power brokers while forging connections with a new Catholic elite, who were increasingly calling the shots. Charles's 1830 visit coincided with the build-up to the general election. He expressed interest in becoming a candidate and solicited the support of Lord Leitrim.[4] The Clements family, however, had wrested political control from the St Georges and were unwilling to relinquish their hold. Lord Leitrim furnished a non-committal response and Charles was forced to abandon his political aspirations. His withdrawal, however, was not without consequences, as his tenants uncharacteristically 'disregarded his instructions' and Lord Robert Bermingham Clements was defeated by a margin of six votes.[5] St George continued to participate in local politics and, as proprietor of the county town, he availed of the status it entailed and attempted to exercise control with subtle, if at times vengeful diplomacy. Having failed to gain Lord Leitrim's endorsement, St George turned instead to local government competing to serve alongside his Catholic countrymen in positions which had formerly been his family's preserve.[6]

In August 1836 Ireland's pro-Catholic lord lieutenant, the earl of Mulgrave, embarked on a tour of the country. On Tuesday 23 August Mulgrave arrived in Carrick where his visit was described with biased disparity by the local press. The *Roscommon Journal* claimed that his excellency was met by St George's tenants on the boundary of the estate and escorted through several 'tastefully decorated' archways to the courthouse, were St George presented a welcoming address.[7] In contrast, an anonymous correspondent writing for the *Roscommon and Leitrim Gazette* criticized the 'miserable scare-crow arches', the barren estate and St George's failure to attend the event due to a convenient bout of ill-heath. Calling to task an 'excellent landlord

7. Charles Manners St George, 1840, by Maria Rohl
(National Library of Sweden, KB1725937)

and patriotic gentleman [who] values too much the pleasures of a foreign land', the writer challenged St George 'to spend a thought on the improvement of the dirty acres which give him the means of enjoying these pleasures'.[8] Two months later, as Charles prepared to sojourn in warmer climes, the inhabitants of Carrick assembled in the courthouse. Speaking on their behalf, Captain Cox appealed to St George to live among his tenants and redress the impact of his protracted absences and the actions of a non-resident agent. The gauntlet had been forcibly thrown down. Professing to be 'thrilled through every fibre of his heart', St George found it 'impossible to resist' their request and 'pledged to spend the greater part of his life in the bosom of his ... tenantry'.[9] St George spent protracted and well-timed periods in Carrick but, despite a second deputation accompanied by over two hundred signatures, he did not maintain a permanent residence on the estate until 1849.[10] In 1842, Captain Cox reaped his reward and was appointed agent of the Carrick estate.

St George was an eloquent speaker whose tendency to over-entertain a captive audience prompted criticism that 'Charlo, forgetting what was due to Manners, would not suffer one gentleman to say a word'.[11] His desire to take the floor, however, provided ample opportunity for the public engineering of his actions. In 1838, having been proposed by George Peyton and seconded by Francis O'Beirne, St George chaired an anti-poor-law meeting in Carrick courthouse. He criticized a system of government that allowed a country to export 'the bulk of her own produce while the most of her population can scarcely purchase with the proceeds of that export, their daily potato'.[12] He spoke out against the cost and futility of a workhouse system, the support of which he argued would 'fall exclusively on the landed interest, consigning a still larger number to starvation'. Espousing the dual qualities of 'system and economy', he called for improved agricultural practices and an end to ostentation, the exercising of which had, ironically, played a large part in the rise and near demise of the St George dynasty. O'Beirne praised the extent of St George's research and talent but reminded the esteemed gentleman that he also had the power and the resources to put his fine words into action.

In 1839, having curried Catholic favour, St George attempted to cover all bases. Chairing a meeting in the town, he vouched for the millions of Irish subjects 'who would shed the last drop of their blood' in defence of their 'beloved queen'.[13] In anticipation of the meeting, an anonymous inhabitant put pen to paper and advised St George that his attentions could have been employed 'with far more propriety' in consideration of his 'starving brethren'.[14] The inhabitant stressed that 'property has its duties as well as its rights' and, having pulled the proverbial strings, waited for the good gentleman to react. Rising to the bait, St George thanked the writer for his interest, donated £50 for the relief of the distressed poor and gave directions for a new road through the estate.[15] Whether driven by conscience, coercion or economics, St George appears to have had the interests of

his tenants at heart. Believing wholly in the merits of the practices he
endorsed, his actions were systematic and driven by sound economic
principles. He was prepared to invest time, effort and money but
expected his ventures to be self-perpetuating with potential for
financial gain. Faced with a neglected estate and a town that did
not 'present the appearance of wealth … nor exhibit the marks of
progressive improvement', St George set about using local labour to
deliver the infrastructures that it was hoped would allow the town
and its hinterland to thrive.[16] He procured a patent for six additional
fairs and, whereas at Headford the waiving of market tolls was
considered a commercial inducement, Charles chose to reintroduce
the charges and invest the proceeds in the facility.[17] In 1837 he
established a library and reading room in the town to promote literary
and agricultural knowledge. Access was subject to a subscription of
2d. per month.[18] The same year, at risk of being regarded 'a snarling
censor of accustomed enjoyments', he founded a Carrick branch of
the Temperance Society.[19] He was chairman of the Carrick Loan
Fund and paid very close attention to the feasibility of the projects it
funded. He backed the works of the Shannon Navigation Commission
and provided 'without remuneration' all premises in his possession.[20]
He actively supported a national railway service, and was chairman
of the General Irish Railway Committee and a member of the Great
Western Railway Committee.[21] He campaigned for a Carrick branch
of the London and Dublin Bank, which opened in 1844.[22] Despite his
efforts, on the eve of the Great Famine, the town of Carrick remained
unpaved, was badly lit and boasted 'little in the way of appearance
that is prepossessing'.[23] Its owner, its people and its infrastructures
were about to be put to the test.

THE GREAT FAMINE

In September 1845 outbreaks of blight on the east coast were followed
by an announcement that 'the potato murrain has unequivocally
declared itself in Ireland'.[24] The circumstances which contributed
to the extent of the calamity were a complex amalgamation of
actions and reactions, driven by ideological conviction and media-
fuelled public opinion. Couched in moralist dogma and impeded by
bureaucratic delays, official relief measures were generally inadequate,

too slow and subject to unrealistic conditions.[25] Despite public condemnation, the Poor Relief Act was passed in 1838.[26] Delivered by a network of workhouses, it introduced an indoor relief system designed to meet ordinary levels of distress. Built to house 800 inmates, Carrick workhouse opened its doors in July 1842, supporting a population of 67,000 people.[27] It occupied a four-acre site at Gallows Park, leased by St George for £21 2s. 8d. per annum. A further three acres in the adjoining townland of Lisnabrack were set aside for use as a graveyard, netting St George an additional £10 3s. 6d. annually.[28] The workhouse dominated the socio-economic landscape of Carrick, providing support, economic opportunity and an influx of desperate people that far outweighed the resources of the community.

In November 1845 a Temporary Relief Commission was established, tasked with orchestrating the formation and management of local-relief committees. Leitrim's deputy lieutenant complained of the difficulties involved in forming appropriate committees due to the absence of resident gentry.[29] Despite the problems encountered, Carrick Relief Committee was eventually established in April 1846, consisting of prominent landholders and nine members of the local clergy. St George was represented by his agent Captain Charles Cox.[30] The construction of Carrick bridge and quays had been sanctioned prior to the onset of blight (fig. 8). Throughout 1845, it ensured a continuous demand for labour, with on average 2,260 persons employed daily.[31] Farmers, however, were said to have struggled to compete with the 'liberal rates of pay' offered and the shortage of available labour.[32] By early 1846, works were nearing an end and employment figures had fallen to 412 persons per day.[33]

In March 1846 the Board of Works was made responsible for temporary relief work.[34] The sum of £1,600 was granted to Carrick Union and additional works were authorized by the Shannon Navigation Commission.[35] Carrick Relief Committee was accused of neglecting its duties and failing to supply lists of persons eligible for work. Carrick bank was unable to dispense sufficient coinage to meet the weekly wage bill, the demand for provisions soared and prices charged in the town far outweighed money earned on the works. The output of 'half-famished' workers impacted performance-based rates of pay and wages were mortgaged to 'tommy-shops' where workers were expected to commit part of their earnings or receive goods in lieu.[36] In February 1847 the scheme was abandoned. In the townland of Moyglass, Co. Roscommon, which had been purchased by John Keogh in 1790, the distressed workmen of the of the vicinity pleaded for 'work and nothing but work' before being compelled to 'break the ties of honesty' with which they were bred.[37] With mortality rates increasing dramatically, the government was forced to forgo economic ideologies and in February 1847 the Temporary Relief (Soup Kitchen) Act was passed.[38] Public works in Carrick Union had ceased by the end of March, but it was a further six weeks before the promised government kitchens were operational, supplying food to up to 32,000 persons per day.[39] By early 1847 Carrick workhouse was hopelessly overcrowded and disease was rife. In an appeal to the Poor-Law Commission, the parish priest described how there had been '189 deaths in March, 295 in April … until the house literally emptied itself into the graveyard'.[40] The Poor-Law Amendment Act 1847 made provision for outdoor relief, but was subject to the controversial 'Gregory clause', which stipulated that occupiers of more than one-quarter acre were not entitled to aid.[41] On New Year's Eve, over six months after the act had been passed, Carrick Union received authorization to grant outdoor relief to the able-bodied.[42] By that time, over 1,600 persons were said to have given up their land in anticipation of aid and were roaming the Union without shelter.[43]

The Poor-Law system was funded by a tax on property valued at £4 or more. In addition, public-work schemes were paid for in whole or in part by loans recoverable from county cess.[44] Throughout the Union, rate collectors were subjected to intimidation and it was reported that 'every gentleman's door was shut against them and they received no rates except from the poorest classes'.[45] By 1848 poor rates for the Carrick Union were £8,209 in arrears and it was one of twenty-two unions officially designated as distressed.[46] That spring, in Carrick Union, only one-fifth of the normal potato acreage was planted and blight struck again.[47] The following year, two-thirds of the crop was saved and over the next three years harvests gradually returned to normal. Finally in September 1853 it was announced that 'the potato is ripening naturally, free from blight and will be more than an average crop'.[48]

Rentals and accounts for the Carrick estate cover the years 1842–71, but do not include the period May 1847–April 1850.[49] No

8. Carrick-on-Shannon bridge, 2020 (photograph by Mark Kelly)

documentation survives to address this deficit. A comparative analysis of the rentals for the years commencing May 1846 and May 1850 allows some understanding of the estate's management to be afforded and the repercussions of the Famine to be considered.[50] Faced with the fatal disparity between government relief policy and the reality of outcomes achieved, individuals and private charities struggled to fulfil official obligations and address the inevitable shortfalls. By 1847, Catholic priests had been excluded from relief committees and landlord participation limited. The exclusion of the priests fuelled sectarian animosity, while the reduction of landlord involvement antagonized persons whose well-intentioned exertions were crucial to the relief effort. During the early years of the Famine, enthusiastic attempts were made to provide support, but as the years dragged on, many were overcome by the scale of the disaster or became desensitized to the plight of those around them.

On the St George estate, direct lessees were mainly strong farmers or merchants with commercial enterprises based in the town. Most survived the Famine and many profited from the opportunities it presented. In an environment in which survival was paramount, lines were crossed, actions justified and across all levels of society people behaved in ways they might later prefer to forget. Alexander Faris of Shannon Lodge forgave all rent for the duration of the

Famine, an action that may have led him to surrender over half of his holding.[51] William Cunningham, a local undertaker, was paid on average £15 per month for the supply of coffins to the workhouse.[52] He also supplemented his income carrying immigrating inmates to the train station in Mullingar.[53] By 1850 Cunningham had leased five development plots in the town as well as part of the lands relinquished by Faris. The Bournes family were strong farmers whose association with the estate can be traced back to 1780.[54] Robert Bournes was contracted to supply potatoes and corn to the workhouse. The magnitude of this endeavour is evidenced by the legal remedies taken to recover arrears of £1,800, with settlement eventually agreed following threats to seize workhouse property.[55] Bournes also provided stone from his quarry and reinvented himself as a paving contractor. By 1851 he had acquired the leases on ten additional holdings, making him the largest tenant on the estate. In 1846 Neil Tunney took possession of a drapery shop on Main Street. Despite the extreme poverty endured by a large sector of the population, the demand for luxury fashion items coupled with the sale of 'a large selection of blankets, suitable for charitable purposes', allowed Tunney to lease two further premises in the town.[56] Architect Robert Robinson, whose building projects formed part of St George's plan to regenerate the town, was one of several property owners who rented rooms by the week. Tenants were frequently unable to meet their commitments and a continuous cycle of rentals and ejectments is evidenced in the court registers.[57] The fear of disease was also a barrier to charitable behaviour. In April 1849 Robinson's property was secured by the Poor-Law Guardians for use as an auxiliary workhouse.[58] The following month actions were taken against the occupiers of ten adjacent properties charged with allowing dung heaps to accumulate on their premises. These nuisances were most likely deliberately created, reflecting the attitude of a local community hardened by famine fatigue.[59] With an increased demand for their services, some local-government employees and staff engaged by St George also improved their lot. The local sheriff, his bailiff, the poor-rate collector and a caretaker on the estate all increased their holdings. In 1846, Richard Threlfall, St George's bailiff, received an annual salary of £12 and a sizeable Christmas bonus 'as an encouragement to the performance of his duties ... which have been very arduous this year'.[60] By 1850, Threlfall's earnings had increased to £30 annually and the family subsequently opened a pawnbroker's office on Bridge Street.[61]

Carrick petty-sessions order books record numerous thefts of turnips or cabbages from farms on the estate. In many cases fines were waived on the understanding that the defendant would not reoffend, but as the Famine progressed, more hard-line tactics appear to have been adopted and increasing penalties enforced. In some instances, the nature of items stolen suggests that, faced with death by starvation, incarceration or transportation were the intended outcomes. This may have been the motivation for 18-year-old Thomas McGaherty who, having been arrested for stealing a scarf from Tunney's shop, was transported for ten years.[62] Workers filed for payment of outstanding wages and actions frequently involved employers who tended to serially offend.[63] The high cost of provisions led to an escalation in violent behaviour and outbreaks of public disorder.[64] An incendiary device was thrown at the courthouse, bricks were hurled through rooming-house windows and proprietors were taunted with threatening language.[65] The sale of firearms remained constant and instances of agrarian unrest were common with persons taking possession of vacated properties targeted by local gangs.[66] In April 1846 the home of Michael Padian was attacked by armed men demanding the return of land formerly held by Padian's uncle, who had been forced to enter the workhouse. Padian vacated the property and, in a convenient turn of events, St George paid £59 13s. 10d. to purchase back the land and subsequently recouped his outlay from a co-party to the lease.[67] A similarly motivated attack was directed at Patrick McGrievy, a bailiff and occupier of a mid-sized farm who had increased his holding in 1847. Four armed men, reported to be a 'gang of Rockites', called to his home and his son was shot. Exhibiting the extent to which the community had become riven by the politicization of perceived grievances, a local man was convicted of the murder and sentenced to death.[68]

The enforced sale of the Carrick estate had significantly reduced its size but the property was debt free and, compared with many of his contemporaries, St George was better positioned to survive the impending crisis. In 1846 the estate was divided into 309 plots. Due to the limited nature of the plot descriptors, it is not possible to accurately

differentiate between urban and agricultural holdings.[69] Between
1768 and 1846, despite an 80 per cent reduction in the acreage of the
estate, the total number of plots had almost doubled, evidencing the
dramatic increase in the population and the level of pressure exerted
on the land. By May 1850 the number of lease holders had reduced
to 208 compared to 247 in 1846.[70] Plot numbers remained relatively
consistent with 221 tenancies continuing unaltered. Existing lessees
increased their holdings by the addition of 49 vacated lots and the
remaining 39 lots were acquired by tenants not previously recorded
in the ledgers. The 1850 rentals specified provision for a 20 per cent
rental reduction but the actual discount allowed equated to only
33 per cent of the expected figure. A newspaper article published
in October 1849 cited St George's intention to exclude middlemen
from any abatement allowed.[71] This may account for the shortfall and
provide some indication of the extent of rental income derived from
tenants who sublet all or a portion of their holdings. In May 1850 the
total rent debited in respect of the Carrick estate was £2,570, only
5 per cent less than the figure charged in 1846. Despite the rigours
of the Famine, payments received amounted to £2,253. After the
deduction of expenses, from a combined rental income of £6,316
collected across all estates in his possession, St George made a profit
of £2,450.

Whereas most newspapers spoke favourably of St George's actions,
an article written in December 1846 alleged that he had evicted
several tenants and that 'a poor woman was processed for a balance
of 3s. 5d.'[72] As with all allegations or commendations, it is difficult
or impossible to determine the true version of events and one can
only speculate based on the body of available evidence. Examination
of the rentals and a tenants' improvements register maintained from
1850 onwards provide some record of the actions taken by St George
during the Famine years.[73] The only direct reference to the disaster
was made in January 1847 when it was noted that the rent on two
con-acre plots had been written off due to the total failure of the
potato crop. There is no record of any evictions during the 1846 rental
period, but five ejections were carried out in 1850 and several induced
surrenders occurred during both terms (table 4). In all five ejections,
the lessees were deceased and the extension conditions had expired.
In May 1850 a repossessed property at Portaneoght was re-leased

subject to 20 per cent rental reduction. In November the same year a holding in Cortober was reoccupied, with no change in the rent charged. By May 1851 St George had secured a 50 per cent increase in respect of a larger farm at Cortober but vacated plots in the town remained untenanted.[74] In August 1850 nineteen squatters occupying lands at Cortober received compensation in return for leaving peacefully and levelling their own cabins. The named parties do not appear in the rentals but they may have been sub-tenants on the farms where the 1850 evictions occurred. Three further squatters received similar payment in respect of temporary huts located adjacent to the workhouse. St George also contributed to the emigration costs of tenants who were prepared to vacate their holdings. Amounts paid were generally proportionate to the rent charged and the destination specified. The cost of a deck fare from Sligo to Liverpool was approximately six shillings, while passage to America started at around £3 for steerage accommodation.[75] In 1846, St George paid poor rates in respect of sixty unspecified holdings valued at under £4. By 1850 this number had reduced to fifty. The rental evidence suggests that there was no overriding policy to orchestrate such departures and surrenders, where they occurred, generally benefited both parties to the arrangement.

During the famine years, St George contributed in a measured fashion to official relief programmes but focused his attention on a slow and systematic attempt to address the socio-economic development of the estate. In 1846 St George donated £15 to the dispensary, £30 to the Carrick soup kitchens and £5 towards the salary of an agricultural instructor. He subscribed £50 to the Carrick Relief Committee along with £50 which was advanced as a loan. Drainage works were carried out at several locations and in addition to the reimbursement of costs, tenants were entitled to incorporate reclaimed lands into their existing holdings.[76] Building and renovation works were encouraged, with the cost of construction recoverable on completion. The police barracks was renovated, the church tower was restored and an ornate railing was erected around the courthouse and market square. St George appears to have advanced loans of up to £1,500 to persons willing to engage in development projects. Recipients of such advances included Captain and Robert Cox, whose ventures included a large house beside the courthouse.

This property was purchased by St George in 1849 and became his principal residence.[77] Originally named Hillsberry, the imposing Italianate mansion was subsequently named Hatley Manor (fig. 9), reaffirming connection to the ancestral home in Cambridgeshire and continuing the tradition initiated by his forbears at Corsparrow.[78] In 1850 St George commissioned the emblazonment of the family crest on the front of Church's Hotel. His action was a blatant declaration of the St Georges' part in the creation and preservation of a legacy the embodiment of which was Carrick town.

Whereas St George and the inhabitants of the estate all played a part in its survival, rentals, official reports and media coverage fail to convey the scale and momentum of a crisis that far outweighed their ability to cope. Between 1841 and 1851, in the townlands that formed part of the St George estate, over one thousand people died or were displaced (table 5). This represents a decline of 28 per cent compared to an overall reduction of 30 per cent across the combined populations of Cos Leitrim and Roscommon.[79] The population of the town fell by 31 per cent, while in the predominantly agricultural areas a reduction of 24 per cent was noted. Town Parks, on the outskirts of the town, saw a substantial increase in population, evidence of the influx of persons seeking work or famine relief. Throughout the Carrick estate, the number of occupied houses fell by 155 but with only twenty-two uninhabited houses as opposed to fourteen in 1841 – the imprint of no fewer than 147 families was erased from the landscape by the rapid levelling of their homes. At Headford, in the absence of his older brother Richard, Stepney St George worked tirelessly to assist those in distress. In May 1847 he died of fever 'caught in the discharge of his arduous duties as chairman of Headford Relief Committee'.[80] Notwithstanding the family's efforts, the population of Headford town declined by 26.6 per cent, testament to the insurmountable nature of the crisis.[81]

'IT IS FINISHED'

In the wake of the Famine, the inhabitants of Carrick town and estate struggled to get back on their feet and come to terms with the catastrophic events that had decimated their community. St George

Table 4. Ejectments and surrenders, Carrick estate, 1846 and 1850

Name	Year	Status	Plot	Inducement
Henry McManess	1846	leave peaceably	Drishogues	£3 10s. to emigrate with family to England
Thomas Foley	1846	leave peaceably	Attyfinlay	£6 to emigrate with family to England
Reps Terence Reynolds	1850	expired lease	Portaneoght	ejected
Bridget Reynolds	1850	squatter	Portaneoght	£4 to send daughter to America
Michael Reynolds	1850	squatter	Portaneoght	£5 to emigrate to America
Reps John Clifford	1850	expired lease	Cortober	ejected
Reps John O'Brien	1850	expired lease	Cortober	ejected
Reps Michael McGarry	1850	expired lease	Plot town	ejected
Reps John Kelly	1850	expired lease	Plots town	ejected
William Smith	1850	leave peaceably	Attirory	£10 to emigrate with family to America
Richard Smith	1850	leave peaceably	Attirory	£10 to send son and daughter to America
Pat Higgins	1850	squatter	Cortober	10s.
James Salmon	1850	squatter	Cortober	10s.
Thomas Duignan	1850	squatter	Cortober	10s.
Bessy O'Neill	1850	squatter	Cortober	10s.
Honore Moran	1850	squatter	Cortober	10s.
Owen Morahan	1850	squatter	Cortober	10s.
John Duignan	1850	squatter	Cortober	10s.
Andy Kelly	1850	squatter	Cortober	10s.
John Kelly	1850	squatter	Cortober	10s.
John Conlon	1850	squatter	Cortober	10s.
Peter O'Brien	1850	squatter	Cortober	10s.
Pat Kelly	1850	squatter	Cortober	10s.
James Murray	1850	squatter	Cortober	10s.
Catherine Kelly	1850	squatter	Cortober	10s.
H. Clare	1850	squatter	Cortober	7s. 6d.
C. Grey	1850	squatter	Cortober	7s. 6d.
M. Byrne	1850	squatter	Cortober	7s. 6d.
John McGrievy	1850	squatter	Cortober	10s.
Pat Powell	1850	squatter	Cortober	10s.
Margaret Foord	1850	squatter	Gallows Park	10s.
Anne Logan	1850	squatter	Gallows Park	10s.
James Brady	1850	squatter	Gallows Park	10s.

(source: St George 1846 and 1850 rentals (NLI, MS 4005–6))

9. Hatley Manor, 2023
(photograph courtesy of the National Inventory of Architectural Heritage)

opened the doors of Hatley Manor and entertained with lavish style.[82] The fair green, which detracted from his view of the river, was relocated to a 'commodious and well-situated site' at the eastern end of the town.[83] In its place, St George built a park, which, being designated for the 'recreation and amusement' of his tenants, fulfilled a mutually beneficial function.[84] He commissioned a promenade at 'very large expense' and invited proposals for the construction of houses in the town and a communal boat slip on the quay.[85] In June 1852 St George returned to Carrick having wintered in Florence due to his failing health. Bonfires blazed throughout the estate and its inhabitants were said to have turned out in force to celebrate his safe return. Reporting on their arrival, a journalist waxed lyrically about the 'good feeling between the proprietor and his tenantry at a time when the class war between these parties seems to endanger the very existence of society'.[86] Veiled by poetic optimism and journalistic bias, however, deep resentment festered. The disparate lifestyles of those who had prospered and those who had barely managed to stay alive were a constant reminder of a devastating experience that some sought to avenge and others tried to eradicate or forget.

By 1852, driven by a manipulative election campaign, social tensions were fuelled by sectarian conflict rooted in perceived accountability

Table 5. Population and occupied houses, Carrick estate, 1841 and 1851

	Townland	Statute acres	Population			Occupied houses		
			1841	1851	% decline	1841	1851	% decline
Carrick town	Town	–	1716	1100	36	208	149	28
	Gaol	–	–	88	–	–	–	–
	Infirmary	–	–	44	–	–	–	–
	Workhouse	–	–	552*	–	–	–	–
	Cortober	–	268	134	50	45	24	47
Leitrim	Attifinlay	79	99	70	29	17	13	24
	Attirory	245	104	67	36	16	10	38
	Ballynamony	99	69	54	22	12	10	17
	Cloonfeacle	60	31	27	13	6	5	17
	Cloonsheerevagh	54	86	49	43	14	7	50
	Cloonsheebane	74	23	25	-9	4	4	0
	Correen	193	121	19	84	19	6	68
	Corryolus	157	78	19	76	16	2	88
	Drummagh	80	70	57	19	11	7	36
	Grove	9	7	5	29	1	1	0
	Hartley	253	20	11	45	3	2	33
	Lisnabrack	42	29	7	76	5	1	80
	Lisnagat	43	39	10	74	5	1	80
	Portaneoght	78	20	9	55	4	1	75
	Town Parks	289	195	345	-77	31	52	-68
Roscommon	Ardglass (pt owned)	254	122	66	46	21	11	48
	Cortober	183	163	105	36	26	15	42
	Drishoge	79	80	85	-6	13	16	-23
	Knockananima	100	52	39	25	8	9	-13
	Macnadille	114	85	71	16	15	13	13
	Toormore	116	100	78	22	19	13	32
	Cloonmaan	93	43	36	16	5	6	-20
	Cloonskeeveen	133	106	83	22	19	14	26
	Tullyleague	96	81	52	36	14	10	29

(sources: *Census of Ireland for the year 1851. Part I. Showing the area, population and number of houses by townland an electoral division. County of Leitrim*, 89–114 [1548], HC 1852–3, xcii, 427–52; *County of Roscommon*, 179–216 [1555], HC 1852–3, xcii, 517–56. *persons residing in the workhouse have been excluded from all calculations relating to this table)

and deflection of blame. The situation was exacerbated by the passing of the 1850 Franchise Reform Act, which saw the Leitrim electorate increase from 554 to 1,265.[87] Most voters were tenant farmers seeking tenurial security and compensation for improvements made to their holdings. Their grievances, which were championed by the Irish Tenant League, were especially pertinent in the context of the sale of insolvent estates facilitated by the Encumbered Estates Act 1848.[88] Embittered by anti-landlord sentiment, St George, having made a political U-turn, proposed the Conservative candidate Hugh Lyons Montgomery. Charles Clements, the sitting Liberal member, was nominated by Francis O'Beirne. Dr John Brady of Cavan received the Tenant League endorsement. On the day that the candidates were announced, an angry mob, reputedly incited by the priests, gathered on the streets of Carrick. Viscount William Sydney Clements, having quelled the demonstration, received a public declaration of gratitude signed by St George and forty-two inhabitants of the town.[89] Montgomery topped the poll and, despite having no political presence in the county, Brady's tenant-rights endorsement secured him the second seat. Charles Clements's defeat marked the end of a political hegemony that had lasted for more than eighty years.[90] St George was commended for his 'frank enunciation of true Protestant principles' and the 'fearless and independent part' he had played in securing a Conservative victory.[91] In his response, displaying the extent of his bitterness, he spoke of 'the torrent of infidelity and disloyalty which was insidiously sapping the foundations of society'.[92] Abandoning any semblance of diplomacy, he lashed out at 'that all grasping popery which embolden by ... non-resistance ... wade[s] through blood to its own sole aggrandizement'.[93]

In October 1852, as the breach between Catholics and Protestants widened, St George made the ill-timed decision to discontinue support for the local national school. He was condemned from the altar as a 'Sasenach Heretic' and the earlier address made to Viscount Clements was posted on the chapel gates along with an appeal to Leitrim's Catholics to withdraw all custom from the listed parties.[94] The local curate was arrested and charged with Whiteboyism. He appeared at Carrick court the following December, before magistrates John Peyton, Lindsay Birchall and Charles Cox.[95] After a lengthy examination of the witnesses, the case was adjourned and, perhaps anxious to limit the damaging effects of the trial, Cox declined to take any further part in the action. The case was eventually dropped, but the battle lines had been drawn and in the 'class war' between landlord and tenant, religion was again at the core.[96]

Faced with a deep-seated mutual resentment, St George was no longer prepared to fund events over which he did not exercise control. Like Lord Forbes over twenty-five years earlier, he was forced to acknowledge his part in a process that appeared not be in his best interest. Pleading ill health, it is alleged that he chose to maintain a 'respectful distance' by spending his remaining years in Florence.[97] Notwithstanding his supposed stance, St George travelled to Carrick most summers, but his social and political interactions were minimal. Having reached a stalemate, his visits were greeted with outward enthusiasm and rewarded with the usual hospitality. In 1851 at a ball held at Hatley Manor, St George introduced Victor Sabro Levy de l'Hérault of France, upon whose services he was to increasingly rely.[98] The Frenchman resided at Hatley Manor and with suave sophistication became the public, albeit not so popular, face of the increasingly fragile St George. Cox resigned in 1860 and was replaced by William Lawder of Ballinamore.[99] In March 1862 l'Hérault and bailiff Richard Threlfall received threatening notices signed 'Molly Maguire'. Putting aside their difference, St George's tenants emphatically renounced the action and 112 named persons contributed £481 10s. as a reward for information leading to the writer's conviction.[100] Whereas the threats were rooted in anti-landlord sentiment, the reaction of the tenants helped to bridge the mutually 'respectful distance' that for over ten years had shaped estate dynamics. In July 1863, following a protracted absence, St George made what was to be his last visit to Carrick. In their welcoming address, his 'devoted and happy tenantry' assured him of their lasting commitment to the town.[101] In response, St George acknowledged the 'prosperous and independent position so peculiar to the Hatley Manor estate' and conceded that however well-intentioned the efforts of a landlord might be, such a successful outcome could not have been achieved without the 'zealous cooperation' of his tenants.[102] A truce had been reached.

Notwithstanding the tensions that detracted from their efforts, Charles St George and all persons associated with the estate were a community within which complex relationships and choreographed actions contributed to mutually beneficial outcomes. Building on the legacy of the self-styled Sir George of Carrickdrumrusk, together they created a town that in 1846 boasted 'little in the way of appearance' but emerged from the Famine with the 'desirable appendages to a well-regulated town'.[103] Charles St George died in Florence on 22 November 1864. His widow inherited the estate and, as the couple had no children, following Ingri's death in March 1873 it passed to her niece Petronella.[104] Charles's body was brought back to Carrick and in 1865 was laid to rest in a mausoleum in the grounds of Hatley Manor.[105] Overlooking what was once the 'gateway to the west', his final resting place memorializes a dynastic association that, having gone full circle, had ended at the point at which it had begun. In Carrick church, an elaborate marble monument surmounted by the family crest proclaims his ancient lineage.[106] Encapsulating the conflicting social and economic realities of a legacy that was over two centuries in the making, a central plaque records his last words: 'It is finished'.

Conclusion

This study illustrates how, over the course of 250 years, a 'wild and unhaunted wasteness' became a well-run profitable estate encompassing the shire town of Co. Leitrim.[1] It demonstrates the key roles played by the St George family as agents of Ireland's colonization and the extent to which their participation in the anglicization process reshaped the physical and cultural landscape of their Carrick estate. Examination of six generations of the St George family has allowed the process to be assessed relative to their social advancement and the turbulent political environment in which it was achieved. The parallel analysis of native and settler communities shows how the inherent fighting spirit that propelled Carrick natives to be among the 'first out in action and last in submission' impacted the pace and scope of the transformation.[2] Comparisons were made between the family's Carrick and Headford estates at key stages in their development. Both underwent a similar process of change driven by similar motivations and exposures. Specific outcomes were impacted by the timing of an event relative to the capacity of the estate and its people at a particular point in time. The continuous sequence of actions and reactions became blurred over time and the end results were fundamentally the same.

The advancement of the St Georges' wealth and status and the processes through which they were achieved were not dissimilar to those orchestrated by many 'reduced' families who took advantage of the opportunities offered in Ireland.[3] With the inflation of honours causing a decline in respect for the peerage, their apparently indisputable genealogy was a 'useful weapon' in the battle for status.[4] To a large extent their advancement was determined by military prowess and their abilities to align themselves with the victor when the battle was won. Conversion of military collateral to land, wealth and status was impacted by the collective endeavours of successive generations. For much of the seventeenth century, the unstable political climate created military opportunities and a bank of land to award the victors. Spurred on by a dogged and at times brutal determination, the St Georges actively participated in a social engineering project designed to wrest power from the indigenous population. They acquired vast tracts of land and were rewarded with lucrative sinecures and titles of honour. The Carrick estate marked their entry into Irish society and throughout the eighteenth century funded the marriages that enabled the descendants of Sir George of Carrickdrumrusk to achieve a level of wealth and status that culminated in an alliance with Ireland's premier peer.

Primogeniture facilitated the transfer of social, economic and political power within the family structure.[5] The way this power was utilized impacted the family's fortunes and the lives of the community within their sphere of influence. Whereas status and the power to enforce change were linked, outcomes were also determined by the actions of individuals whose motivations and prejudices were generally a product of their times. For Sir George St George, unlike most of those rewarded with land during the 1620 Leitrim Plantation, Carrickdrumrusk represented a key component in his quest for advancement. He was actively involved in the development of the estate, which, for most of his life was the family home. He introduced changes that improved the economic potential of the area but were delivered in the context of a corrupt process and the dispossession of the native community. His successor, Baronet Oliver St George, having experienced the atrocities of 1641, actively participated in the zealous administration of the law and capitalized on his military success. Reputedly 'advancing unjust use on unjust use', he increased his personal landholding to more than 14,500 acres.[6] At the time of his death, the anticipated failure of the male line precipitated the creation of a trust that allowed his descendants to extract maximum value from the estate while keeping input to a minimum. When the descendants of Lieut. General St George finally gained possession, they had little interest in a rundown property that had lost its strategic advantage. They mixed in high circles and indulged in the conspicuous consumption that befitted the status to which they aspired. Ultimately, the cost of maintaining their social standing outweighed their financial capacity and the manor of Carrickdrumrusk paid the price.

Leitrim functioned as a gateway to the west and an interprovincial corridor that allowed access between Ulster and Leinster. Located at a fording point of the River Shannon, the former O'Rourke stronghold of *Cora Droma Rúisc* occupied a strategic position that was instrumental in the determination of its fate. On the western banks of the Shannon, the fertile barony of Boyle represented a valuable prize when it came to divvying out the spoils. In terms of the native and Old English population, Catholic freeholders were the primary targets in the drive to reengineer Irish society. The Carrick estate encompassed the former territories of the MacRannalls, McDermotts, Plunketts and Mulloys, who were literally removed from their lands and, depending on their financial ability, charged rent for the privilege of reoccupying it. At the bottom of the social ladder, large numbers of dispossessed Catholics depended on the settler community for their survival. Settlers were reliant on cheap Irish labour for the efficient running of their farms. Whereas Sir Oliver's 1695 trust had contributed to the demise of the estate, the tenurial parity it engendered enabled Catholic and Protestant tenants to co-inhabit the property in circumstances that, by accident rather than design, were more equitable than might have otherwise occurred. Throughout the 250-year timeframe, war, rebellion, possession and dispossession determined the fate of the Carrick estate and the community it supported. Separated by religion and ethnicity, they were bound together by economic dependency and an innate desire to protect the place they regarded as home. Faced with the rapidly changing socio-political landscape, some chose to fight to the bitter end while others sought to navigate the complex interplay of traditions and negotiate beneficial terms. Many of the estate's inhabitants, however, were too poor to influence their circumstances and, caught in the crossfire, they did what was necessary to survive. Reflecting its Gaelic and English origins, Carrickdrumrusk gradually became known as Carrick-on-Shannon, the apparently seamless transition belying the complex history that underpinned its turbulent evolution.

The relaxation of penal legislation coincided with the partial sale of the St George estate, allowing large tracts of land to be transferred to Catholic hands at a pivotal stage in the repeal process. The St Georges' absence combined with a growing Catholic assertiveness saw Carrick develop into a melting pot of religious and political opinions with the main players struggling to keep pace. Charles Manners St George returned to Ireland during the 1830s and for the first time in over seventy-five years a St George was actively involved in the running of the estate. Faced with the consequences of the Great Famine, the estate, its owner and its people were put to the test, but the scale of the disaster far outweighed the capacity of the struggling community. In the townlands that formed part of the estate, over one thousand people died or were displaced and the imprint of almost 150 families was erased by the levelling of their homes. The enforced sale in 1790 ensured the pre-Famine liquidity of the property and for the duration of the crisis it remained financially viable. Using local labour, St George, with the 'zealous cooperation' of his tenantry, slowly but systematically directed the social and economic development of the estate.[7] Notwithstanding the hatred, war and adversity that underpinned its existence, the estate survived and in 1923 passed to the Irish Land Commission. Carrick-on-Shannon, the capital town of Co. Leitrim, survives as a legacy that is a product of its unique position, the actions of its people and the passage of time.

Sir George St George and his descendants

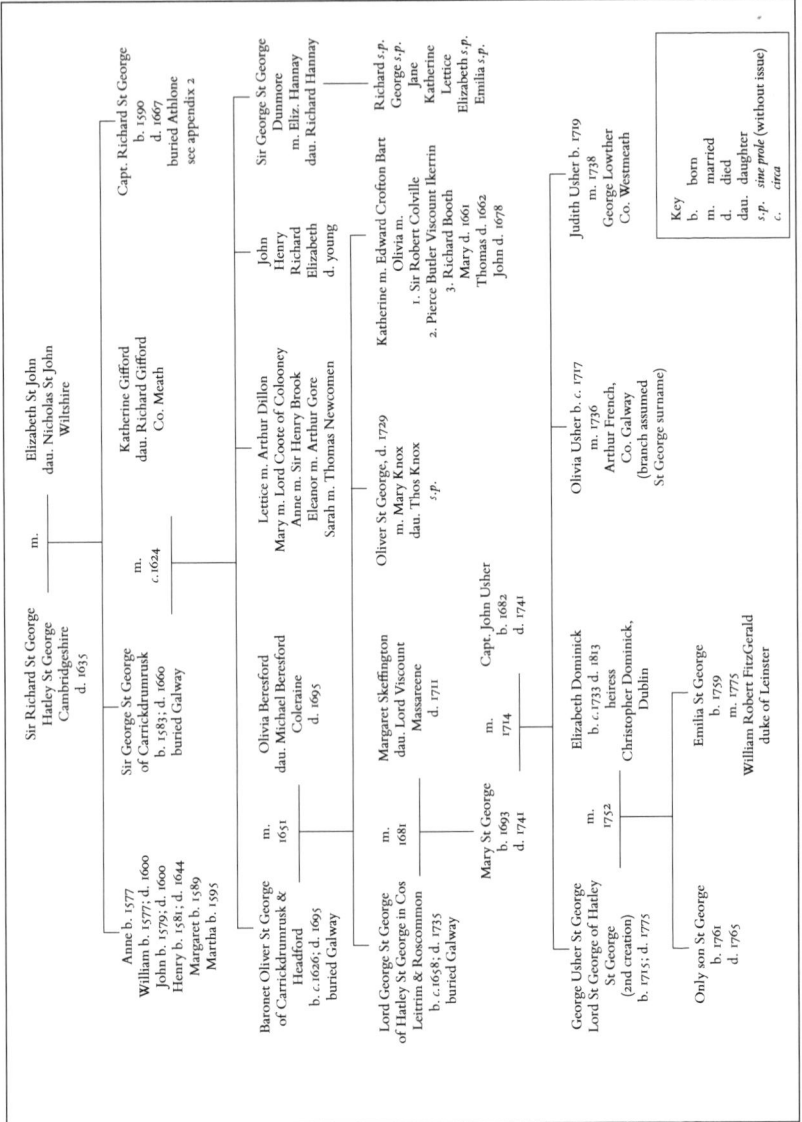

Sir Richard St George
Hadley St George
Cambridgeshire
d. 1635

m.

Elizabeth St John
dau. Nicholas St John
Wiltshire

Capt. Richard St George
b. 1590
d. 1667
buried Athlone
see appendix 2

Sir George St George
of Carrickdrumrusk
b. 1583; d. 1660
buried Galway

m.
c. 1624

Katherine Gifford
dau. Richard Gifford
Co. Meath

Anne b. 1577
William b. 1577; d. 1600
John b. 1579; d. 1600
Henry b. 1581; d. 1644
Margaret b. 1589
Martha b. 1595

Sir George St George
Dunmore
m. Eliz. Hannay
dau. Richard Hannay

Lettice m. Arthur Dillon
Mary m. Lord Coote of Colooney
Anne m. Sir Henry Brook
Eleanor m. Arthur Gore
Sarah m. Thomas Newcomen

John
Henry
Richard
Elizabeth
d. young

Richard s.p.
George s.p.
Jane
Katherine
Lettice
Elizabeth s.p.
Emilia s.p.

Baronet Oliver St George
of Carrickdrumrusk &
Headford
b. c.1626; d. 1695
buried Galway

m.
1651

Olivia Beresford
dau. Michael Beresford
Coleraine
d. 1695

Oliver St George, d. 1729
m. Mary Knox
dau. Thos Knox
s.p.

Katherine m. Edward Crofton Bart
Olivia m.
1. Sir Robert Colville
2. Pierce Butler Viscount Ikerrin
3: Richard Booth
Mary d. 1661
Thomas d. 1662
John d. 1678

Lord George St George
of Hatley St George in Cos
Leitrim & Roscommon
b. c.1648; d. 1735
buried Galway

m.
1681

Margaret Skeffington
dau. Lord Viscount
Massareene
d. 1711

Olivia Usher b. c. 1717
m. 1736
Arthur French,
Co. Galway
(branch assumed
St George surname)

Judith Usher b. 1719
m. 1738
George Lowther
Co. Westmeath

Mary St George
b. 1693
d. 1741

m.
1714

Capt. John Usher
b. 1682
d. 1741

George Usher St George
Lord St George of Hatley
St George
(2nd creation)
b. 1715; d. 1775

m.
1752

Elizabeth Dominick
b. c.1733 d. 1813
heiress
Christopher Dominick,
Dublin

Emilia St George
b. 1759
m. 1775
William Robert FitzGerald
duke of Leinster

Only son St George
b. 1761
d. 1765

Key
b.   born
m.   married
d.   died
dau. daughter
s.p. sine prole (without issue)
c.   circa

(source: St George pedigree (NLI, GO MS 161))

Lieut. General Richard St George and his descendants

Key
b.   born
m.   married
d.   died
dau.   daughter
gdau.   granddaughter
c.   circa
s.p.   sine prole (without issue)
s.p.l.   sine prole legitima (without legitimate issue)

Sir Richard St George
Hatley St George
Cambridgeshire
d. 1635

m.

Elizabeth St John
dau. Nicholas St John
Wiltshire

Capt. Richard St George
b. 1590; d. 1667
buried St Mary's, Athlone

m.
1. 1625
2. c.1644

1. Anne Pinnock
dau. Michael Pinnock
Co. Roscommon
2. Dorothy Moore

Sir George St George
b. 1583; d. 1660
buried Galway
see appendix 1

Mary m. Thomas Ashe
Anne m. Edward Wood
Martha m. Joseph Jackman

Anne b. 1577
William b. 1577; d. 1600
John b. 1579; d. 1600
Henry b. 1581; d. 1644
Margaret b. 1586
Martha b. 1595

Capt. Arthur St George
b. 1629
d. 1702
s.p.

Lt. Henry St George
Sovereign Athlone
b. 1618; d. c.1724
buried St Mary's, Athlone

m.
1669

Anne Hatfield
dau. Ridgley Hatfield
Dublin

Elizabeth Coote
dau. Baron Coote of Coloorey
gdau. Sir George St George
of Carrickdrumrusk
d. 1738

m.
1696

Lt. Gen. Richard St George
Co. Kilkenny
b. c.1670; d. 1755
buried St Mary's, Athlone
s.p.l.

George St George
Co. Kilkenny
m. Elizabeth Bligh
dau. Thomas Bligh, Co Meath

Henry St George
d. c.1724
s.p.

Unknown
partner

Mary Blaydwin
heiress William Blaydwin
b. 1730; d. 1819
buried Bath

Mary St George
b. c.1718

m. 1749

James Mansergh
Co. Cork
b. c.1795
d. c.1774

m.
1788

Anne Stepney
King's Co.
d. c.1792

Richard St George
Carrick-on-Shannon
b. c.1717; d. 1757
buried St Mary's, Athlone

m. 1747

Meleesina Chenevix
dau. Philip Chenevix
heiress b.shop of Lismore
b. 1768; d. 1826

m.
1786

Col. Richard Mansergh
Headford, Co. Galway
assumed surname St George
b. c.1752; d. 1798
buried St Mary's, Athlone

Richard James St George
Headford
b. 1789; d. 1859
m. Elizabeth Shawe
s.p.

Stepney St George
b. c.1790; d. 1847
m. 1. Ann Tyner
m. 2. Frances L'Estrange
buried Headford

Col. Richard St George
Carrick-on-Shannon
b. 1757; d. 1790
buried St Mary's, Athlone

Charles Manners St George
Carrick-on-Shannon
b. 1787; d. 1864
buried Hatley Manor,
Carrick-on-Shannon
s.p.

m.
1827

Ingri Christina Hallberg
dau. Hans Hallberg
Sweden
b. 1798; d. 1873
buried Hatley Manor,
Carrick-on-Shannon

Richard James
St George Headford
b. 1838; d. 1889
m. Mary Henley
buried Headford

Elizabeth b. 1748; d. 1752
Mary Anne m. John Hamilton
Isabella m. John Francis

(source: St George pedigree (NLI, GO MS 161))

Tenants of Carrick estate, 1681 and 1723

	Holding (as cited)	1681 Tenant	Lease Term	Rent £	s.	d.	Holding (as cited)	1723 Tenant	Lease Term	Rent £	s.	d.
Roscommon	Lisloghlin	John Roycroft	21 years	12	0	0	Concrower	Gilbert Roycroft	3 lives	21	0	8
	Lisloghlin (corn mills)	Edward Poors	21 years	22	9	0	Cartron/Lisloghlin (part)?	Francis Waldron	3 lives	13	2	6
	Lacken	not specified	at will	13	10	0	not cited	n/a	-	-	-	-
	Cloonskeevin	not specified	at will	10	0	0	Cloonskeevin	John Henderson	21 years	7	10	10
	Cloonmane						Cloonmane	John Whitham	3 lives	6	6	0
	Clogher	not specified	at will	12	0	0	Clogher	Thomas Lawder	21 years	17	17	0
	Mulloghmore	not specified	at will	20	10	0	Mulloghmore	Edward Winter	at will	21	0	0
	Drumshanco	not specified	at will	18	0	0	Drumshanco Skregg	Charles Cary	3 lives	19	12	6
	Drimcormuck	not specified	at will	6	10	0	Crusnagh (part)	see below	-	-	-	-
	Torymartin	not specified	at will	33	0	0	Torymartin	James Rutledge	3 lives	44	2	8
	Knocknamon Legway Ardleigh						Knockamanon	James and Mary Graham	at will	13	4	8
	Ardcauhil	not specified	at will	6	6	0	Ardcauhil	David Hughes and Edward Thompson	at will	4	11	0
	Kilticunneen	not specified	at will	16	16	0	Kilticunneen	Joseph Roberts and James Gilmore	3 lives	14	2	0
	Killfogna	not specified	at will	16	16	0	Kilfoghna	Robert Stanly	3 lives	23	6	0
	Cargowen	not specified	at will	5	0	0	Gillstown (part)	Thomas Stafford (see below)	-	-	-	-
	Tulloleigh, Knockadaltin	not specified	at will	25	2	0	Tulloleigh	Robert Cary	at will	15	15	0
	Lackagh	not specified	at will	5	0	0	Lackagh	John King esq	3 lives	6	6	0
	Ballimacormuck	not specified	at will	4	0	0	not cited	n/a	-	-	-	-

	1681						1723					
	Holding (as cited)	Tenant	Lease Term	Rent £	s.	d.	Holding (as cited)	Tenant	Lease Term	Rent £	s.	d.
	Corray	not specified	at will	13	0	0	Corry	Edmond Dowell	3 lives	12	12	0
	Cloonragh, Carrowkeel	not specified	at will	12	18	0	Carrowkeel	Dudley Hanly	at will	9	9	9
							Cloonragh	Bridget Connors	21 years	23	10	0
	Knockacarrow	not specified	at will	8	2	0	Boher (part)?	John Plunkett?	21 years	-	-	-
	Cloonmane	not specified	at will	8	0	0	Cloonmane	Luke Dillon	21 years	10	10	0
	Caldragh Togher Carrowmore	not specified	at will	15	4	6	Caldragh	John King esq.	3 lives	42	0	0
	Meeree	not specified	at will	17	10	0	Meeree	Griffith Lloyd	3 lives	23	8	0
	Taulagh Shronkeeragh	not specified	at will	16	10	0	Taulagh	Thomas Gilmore	3 lives	20	18	1
	Ardglass, Mackinedilly Tourmore	not specified	at will	41	7	6	Boher	John Plunkett	21 years	66	1	0
Roscommon	Aghamanan	not specified	at will	4	8	6	Aghamananan	James McDonagh	at will	8	8	0
	Aghakinedy Ardleckney Cashell	not specified	at will	23	7	6	Ardleckney	William Browne	21 years	31	12	8
	Crusnagh Maughes Derryyerry Faunaghdrissagh Aghaletty	not specified	at will	32	0	0	Crusnagh	Daniel McCormuck Garret Jordan part Lord St George	at will	24	10	6
	Knockglass, Knocknacree	Hugh McDermott	21 years	23	5	0	Knockglass	Hugh McDermott	3 lives	27	19	8
	Gillstowne Clonoon, Glann	Thomas Stafford	21 years	26	0	0	Gillstown	Thomas Stafford	3 lives	33	12	0
	Lysanuran Tubberbreedy	Bryan Killaghan	9 years	18	0	0	Lisinnoran	Henry Leneghan	21 years	18	18	0
	Martry, Rinnaridaun Carrowcrin Caldragh	Richard Plunkett	21 years	41	9	0	Caldragh	John King esq.	3 lives	42	0	0
	Ballymacneboy	Richard Plunkett	21 years	14	0	0	Ballymacneboy	Oliver Plunkett	21 years	35	14	0

Leitrim

	1681						1723					
Holding (as cited)	Tenant	Lease Term	Rent £	s.	d.	Holding (as cited)	Tenant	Lease Term	Rent £	s.	d.
Mulloghteige Carrownasse	Darby Leneghan Morris Killaghan	11 years	36	0	0	Mulloghteige	James Eccles	3 lives	57	0	8
Drimercool Ardgrilleen	James Orsen Robert Forester	21 years	26	0	0	Drimercool	Edward Forester	21 years	15	13	6
Moyglass Luggs	Thomas Stafford	21 years	23	0	0	Moyglass	Thady Mahon	3 lives	21	0	0
Clondegagh	George Cary	21 years	20	0	0	Cloonegagh	Lord St George	n/a	0	0	0
Drumkeeran	John Gralton	21 years	23	1	0	Drumkeerin	James Gallagher	3 lives	23	13	0
Cocksparrow	not specified	at will	16	0	0	Cocksparrow	Revd William Howard	at will	26	5	0
Cloonshebane	not specified	at will	12	18	0	Cloonshebane	Lord St George	-	0	0	0
Cloonshereagh	not specified	at will	4	5	0	Cloonshereagh	Lord St George	-	0	0	0
Drumgonnell	not specified	at will	8	13	0	Drumgonnell	Charles Reynolds	at will	4	4	0
Kenoghan						Keenoghan	Terrence McDermott and Richard Stephenson	3 lives	8	8	0
Correen	not specified	at will	10	0	0	Correen	Widow Maloy	at will	23	2	0
Coraughrim	not specified	at will	11	1	0	Coraughrim	Christopher Bridges	at will	14	14	0
Lisseechan	not specified	at will	6	0	0	Lisseechan	James Gallagher	3 lives	11	6	6
Drummagh	not specified	at will	4	0	0	Drummagh	Thomas Griffith	3 lives	11	11	11
Killbodarragh	not specified	at will	4	18	0	Kilboderagh	Richard Stephens and Matt Sanders	3 lives	7	7	0
Drumhalway	not specified	at will	1	10	0	Drumhalway	Hugh Harrod	at will	4	4	0
Cloonfekill	not specified	at will	16	16	0	Cloonfekill	Lawrence Betteridge	3 lives	22	14	0
Cornacarrow	not specified	at will	7	5	0	Cornacarrow					

	1681						1723					
Holding (as cited)	Tenant	Lease Term	Rent £	s.	d.	Holding (as cited)	Tennant	Lease Term	Rent £	s.	d.	
Attyrory (part)	not specified	at will	6	0	0	Attirory	William Miller	at will	8	8	8
						Attirory	John Jones	at will	7	19	0
Attirory (part) Attifenelan	not specified	at will	8	0	0	Attifinnilly	John Redisford	at will	6	16	0
Aghamuny	not specified	at will	10	0	0	Aghamuny	Richard Stephens	3 lives	4	4	0
The 12 Acres and custom of the fairs of Carrick and the bridge of the same	not specified	at will	20	0	0	The 12 Acres	Anne Tweedy	3 lives	3	3	0
							Bryan Cahan	at will	2	10	0
							Luke Cahan	at will	3	0	3
							Alexander Armstrong	at will	3	3	0
							Thomas Hugheston	at will	3	3	0
Fishing weirs	not specified	at will	2	10	0	not cited	n/a	-	-	-	-

(County: Leitrim)

(source: St George v. St George (NLI, p4406))

APPENDIX 4

Inhabitants of Carrick estate in the diocese of Elphin, 1749

Place of abode (as cited)	Inhabitants (surnames as cited)	Total	Religion		Occupations
			Prot.	RC	
Canrawer	**Roycroft** (3) Cunningham Cryan Scott Murray Kelagher Macot Ford (2)	70	18	52	Farmer Cottiers Servants
Clonsheevan	**Walpole Connellan Moran**	26	1	25	Farmers servants
Clonmane	**Whittham**	11	7	4	Farmer Servants
Clogher	Lawder esq Horan Simpson Abraham Conry Beirne (3) McDrury Maxwell McDermot Fitzsimons Gibulan McDonnell Riley Tiernan	91	32	59	Gent Schoolmaster Weaver Smith Cottiers Servants
Mullimore	**Farly Lahy** (2) **Hopkins** (2) **Lavin** (2) **Hilford Danagher Meehan Horan Winter** Ford Loghran **Salmon Kelly Laird** (2) Oats Becket	100	4	96	Farmers Butcher Smith Cottiers Widows
Knockdalton	**Lavin** (4) **Feehley Salmon Greevy Bryan**	46	0	46	Farmers Widows
Scregg	Padin Fox Dans	15	0	15	Cottiers Servant
Torymartin	Leland **Connolly Coveny Naughton** Caslan Lavin Henry	39	4	35	Hatter Farmers Joiners
Knockananima	Warren **Gilmer** Lahy Conaghton	23	4	19	Hatter Farmers Weaver
Ardcouhil	**Thompson** (2) Rogers McGowan	16	11	5	Farmer Weaver Widow Cottier
Kelticuneen	Gilmer Hogg Meehan Cullen Thompson Fannin Leland Hoy	39	28	11	Widow Glover Cottier Weavers Smith Clerk
Kilfaghna	**Stanly** Tearnon Leandon McDermot Roe (2) Brennan McGrivee Crony Frier Linsk	43	8	35	Farmer Labourers
Tullyleige	**Cooper Rutledge Egan Conry Fehy**	25	8	17	Farmers Servant

92

Place of abode (as cited)	Inhabitants (surnames as cited)	Total	Religion Prot.	Religion RC	Occupations
Corry	Connolly Mannin (4) Dowd Kelly (2) Wholan Mulry Leneghan Mullin Lennon Owens Conry	55	0	55	Cottiers
Cloonmane	**Roach Leneghan** (2) **Beirne** (3) <u>Dillon</u> (2)	38	1	37	Farmers Merchant Weaver Quack doctor
Meery	**Jones** <u>**Lloyd**</u> <u>Cox</u> Bealon Lavin Moneen (2) Rourke Borlan McGowan	49	21	28	Farmers Cottiers Widow Taylor
Taulagh	**Rutledge** (2)	9	7	2	Farmer Widow Servants
Ironheragh	**Gilmer** (3)	17	15	2	Farmers
Boher	**Plunkett** (2) McNeal (2) McGreagh Lavin McNamara	41	0	41	Farmer Cottiers Widow Servants
Aghimanane	Hanly Connor Beirne	11	0	11	Cowherd Cottiers
Ardleckny	**Rutledge** Leneghan Gannan Flanagan Roach Blachford <u>Brown</u> Beirne Duffily Lavin	30	1	29	Farmer Cottiers Brog maker Herd
Crusna	Carty Kennedy McCormack **Moran** (2) Murray (2) Bushell Connellan Grier McDermott (4) Dignan	72	9	63	Dealer Farmer Herd Labourer Cottiers
Drumcormack	**Stanly** Linsk (2) Coonan Shannon (2) Carthy	33	8	25	Farmer Cottiers Labourer
Gillstown	<u>Stafford</u> Stafford (2) Kilroy McCormack Gruine Maguire (2) Dockery Lewis Duffy Doolan Guskin King	51	2	49	Gent Cottiers Butcher Widows
Lisnenoran	Lavin Beirne Leneghan (3) McDermot	21	0	21	Cottiers Servant
Martry	Beirne (2) **Harrinton Higgins**	19	0	19	Farmers Widows
Carronaff	Flynn **Keon** Common <u>Cary</u> <u>Adams</u>	27	10	17	Smiths Farmer Apothecary Weaver
Drimernod	**Ford Golrick Foreste**r Dermott <u>Sarce</u> **Rutledge**	38	13	25	Farmers Cooper Widow
Moyglass	**Rutledge** Caring Langham	15	0	15	Farmer Herd Widow

Note: surnames in **bold** described as farmers; surnames <u>underlined</u> recorded as Protestant (source: Legg and Gurrin, *Census of Elphin, 1749*)

Notes

ABBREVIATIONS

Cal. Carew MSS	*Calendar of the Carew manuscripts preserved in the archiepiscopal library at Lambeth, 1515–1623* (6 vols, London, 1867–73)
Cal. Pat. Rolls Ire., Jas I	*[Calendar of] Irish patent rolls, James I* (Dublin, 1830)
Cal. Pat. Rolls Ire., Chas I	*Calendar of patent and close rolls of chancery of Ireland, Charles I, Years 1 to 8.* Ed. James Morrin
Cal. S.P. Ire.	*Calendar of the state papers relating to Ireland* (24 vols, London, 1860–1911)
Census Ire., 1659	Seamus Pender (ed.), *A census of Ireland, circa 1659, with supplementary material from the poll money ordinances, 1660–61* (Dublin, 1939)
CRO	Chief Remembrance Officer
CSO	Chief Secretary's Office
cwt	hundredweight (*centum weight*)
Desid. cur. Hib.	[John Lodge (ed.)], *Desiderata curiosa Hibernica; or A select collection of state papers; consisting of royal instructions, directions dispatches and letters* (2 vols, Dublin, 1772)
HC	House of Commons
ILC	Irish Land Commission
Ir. rec. comm. rep.	*Reports of the commissioners appointed by his majesty to execute the measures recommended in an address of the House of Commons respecting the public records of Ireland; with supplements and appendixes* (3 vols, Dublin, 1811–25)
MSS Carte	Carte manuscripts, Bodleian Libraries, Oxford, MSS 1–279
NAI	National Archives of Ireland
NLI	National Library of Ireland
Ormonde MSS	*Calendar of the manuscripts of the marquess of Ormonde K.P. preserved at Kilkenny Castle* (8 vols, London, 1902–20)
OS	Ordnance Survey
PRO	Public Record Office
RD	Registry of Deeds
TCD	Trinity College Dublin
UCD	University College Dublin

INTRODUCTION

1 *Municipal corporations (Ireland) report, appendix part iii: conclusion of the north-western circuit*, 1015–16 [2629], HC 1836, xxiv, 15–16 (henceforth *Municipal corporations report*).

2 Thomas Lacey, *Sights and scenes in our fatherland* (London, 1863), pp 300–1.

3 Ibid.

4 Ibid.

5 Plantation measurements have been used throughout. One plantation acre equates to approximately 1.62 statute acres.

6 Robert O'Byrne, *Tyrone House and the St George family: the story of an Anglo-Irish family* (Bloomington, 2017).

7 Gerard MacAtasney, *The plantation of County Leitrim, 1585–1670* (Carrick-on-Shannon, 2013); Gerard MacAtasney, *The other famine: the 1822 crisis in Co. Leitrim* (Dublin, 2010); Gerard MacAtasney, 'The dead buried by the dying': the Great Famine in Leitrim (Sallins, 2014); Liam Kelly, *A flame now quenched: rebels and Frenchmen in Leitrim, 1793–98* (Dublin, 1998); Liam Kelly and

Brendan Scott (eds), *Leitrim history and society: interdisciplinary essays on the history of an Irish county* (Dublin, 2019); Richie Farrell, Kieran O'Conor and Matthew Potter (eds), *Roscommon history and society: interdisciplinary essays on the history of an Irish county* (Dublin, 2018).

8 St George v. St George (National Archives Kew, Chancery Masters' Exhibits, C.110 Box 46: NLI, microfilm p4406); St George v. Bruen, concerning lands in Roscommon and Leitrim (NLI, MS 10,079); Maps of the estate of Richard St George in Leitrim and Roscommon, 1768 (NLI, microfilm p2713); Rentals and accounts of the estate of Charles M. St George in Leitrim, Roscommon, Waterford, Tipperary and Offaly, 1842–71 (NLI, MS 4001–22).

9 *Cal. pat. rolls Ire., Jas I; Cal. pat. rolls Ire., Chas I*; 1641 Depositions (TCD, MSS 809–41), available at https://1641.tcd.ie, last accessed 21 Sept. 2022; Books of Survey and Distribution, xiv, Leitrim (NAI, MFS 02/6: NLI, microfilm p3771); R.C. Simington, *Books of survey and distribution: being abstracts of the various surveys and instruments of title, 1636–1703, I: Roscommon* (Dublin, 1949); Marie-Louise Legg and Brian Gurrin (eds), *The census of Elphin, 1749* (Dublin, 2004).

10 Edward Wakefield, *An account of Ireland, statistical and political* (2 vols, Dublin, 1812), ii, p. 614.

I. CREATING THE LEGACY, 1603–91

1 William Kelly (ed.), *Docwra's Derry: a narration of events in north-west Ulster, 1600–4* (Derry, 2003), p. 7.

2 Genealogical notes from ancient calendars, MS Landsdowne 863, fo. 15; *Collectanea topographea et genealogica* (8 vols, London, 1834–43), vi, pp 97–8 at p. 97.

3 'A journal of the lord deputy's into the north', Oct. 1600 (*Cal. S.P. Ire., 1600, Mar.–Oct.*, p. 528); *Collectanea topographea et genealogica*, vi, p. 97.

4 Fenton to Cecil, 3 Oct. 1600 (*Cal. S.P. Ire., 1600, Mar.–Oct.*, p. 465).

5 J.H. Ohlmeyer, *Making Ireland English: the Irish aristocracy in the seventeenth century* (New Haven, CT, 2012), p. 253.

6 Mark Noble, *History of the College of Arms and the lives of kings, heralds and pursuivants from the reign of Richard III until the present time* (London, 1804), p. 236.

7 *Cal. S.P. Ire., 1603–6*, p. 26.

8 Jerrold Casway, 'The last lords of Leitrim: the sons of Sir Teige O'Rourke', *Bréifne Journal*, 7:26 (1988), pp 556–74 at p. 556.

9 Description of Connacht by Sir Oliver St John, 1614 (*Cal. Carew MSS*, vi, p. 295); *Manuscripts Buccleuch and Queensberry*, i, p. 75.

10 *Manuscripts Buccleuch and Queensberry*, i, pp 75–6.

11 Ibid.

12 *Cal. S.P. Ire., 1611–14*, pp 9, 294; *Municipal corporations report*; MacAtasney, *Plantation of Leitrim*, p. 40.

13 Connacht, 1614 (*Cal. Carew MSS*, vi, p. 294).

14 St John to Salisbury, 4 May 1611 (*Cal. S.P. Ire., 1611–14*, p. 47).

15 Victor Treadwell, *Buckingham and Ireland, 1616–28: a study in Anglo-Irish politics* (Dublin, 1998), pp 44–8.

16 Grant to George St George of land in various counties, enrolled 28 June 1620 (NAI, Lodge/4/139–40).

17 *Cal. Carew MSS*, vi, p. 313; Plantation of Leytrim (Marsh's Library, Z4.2.6, pp 476–89); note Mr Lemon (*Cal. S.P. Ire., 1615–25*, p. 265); Lord Deputy to Council, 6 Feb. 1621 (*Cal. S.P. Ire., 1615–25*, p. 313).

18 *Desid. Cur. Hib.*, pp 54, 56, 66.

19 *Cal. S.P. Ire., 1615–25*, pp 285–6.

20 *Cal. S.P. Ire., 1615–25*, pp 292, 422.

21 *Cal. pat. rolls Ire., Jas I*, p. 9; J.J. McDermott, 'Late medieval strongholds of the Gaelic Irish in Co. Leitrim, *c*.1350–1600' in Kelly and Scott (eds), *Leitrim history and society*, pp 103–27 at p. 123.

22 *Cal. pat. rolls Ire., Jas I*, p. 9.

23 *Municipal corporations report*.

24 Matthew Potter, 'Local government in Leitrim, 1585–2014' in Kelly and Scott (eds), *Leitrim history and society*, pp 535–51 at pp 538–9.

25 *Cal. pat. rolls Ire., Jas I*, p. 189.

26 Petition Sir George St George, 18 Nov. 1633 (British Library, Harl. MS 4297, fo. 131) photographically reproduced in MacAtasney, *Plantation of Leitrim*, p. 80.

27 Books of Survey and Distribution, xiv, Leitrim (NAI, MFS 02/6).

28 *Cal. S.P. Ire., 1615–25*, p. 336.

29 Cyril Mattimoe, *North Roscommon: its people and past* (Boyle, 1992), p. 118; Patrick Melvin, 'Roscommon estates and landowners: diversity and durability' in Farrell, O'Conor and Potter (eds), *Roscommon history and society*, pp 327–48 at pp 327–9.

30 Raymond Gillespie, *Seventeenth-century Ireland: making Ireland modern* (Dublin, 2006), pp 79–81.

31 Ibid., p. 81; Simington, *Books of survey and distribution: Roscommon*, pp 74, 149–67.

32 St George estate maps, 1768 (NLI, p2713).

33 OS Name Books for the parish of Kiltoghert, 1836 (www.logainm.ie/en/29163) (29 Sept. 2022).

34 Lords Justices to Privy Council, 22 June 1622 (*Cal. S.P. Ire., 1615–25*, p. 356);

35 Brian Mac Cuarta, 'The Plantation of Leitrim, 1620–41', *Irish Historical Studies*, 12:127 (2001), pp 297–320 at p. 309; 'Certificate of the sixth and last plantation of the county of Leitrim and the small territories of the King's County, Queen's County and Westmeath' in Victor Treadwell (ed.), *The Irish commission of 1622: an investigation of the Irish administration, 1615–1622, and its consequences, 1623–1624* (Dublin, 2006), pp 670–89.

36 Treadwell (ed.), *Irish commission*, pp 675–8, 688.

37 Ibid., pp 688, 732.

38 Mac Cuarta, 'Plantation of Leitrim', pp 310–13.

39 Horatio Smith, 'Translation of an Irish deed of gift', *The Mirror of Literature, Amusement and Instruction*, 13:367 (Apr. 1829), pp 275–7; Treadwell (ed.), *Irish commission*, p. 676.

40 Joseph Meehan, 'Catalogue of the high sheriffs of the county of Leitrim from the year 1605 to the year 1800', *Journal of the Royal Society of Antiquarians of Ireland*, 5th ser., 38:4 (Dec. 1908), pp 382–9 at p. 386; Mac Cuarta, 'Plantation of Leitrim', p. 313.

41 *Cal. S.P. Ire., 1625–32*, p. 139; *Cal. S.P. Ire., 1669–70*, p. 353; *Cal. S.P. Ire.,*

1615–25, p. 285; *Cal. pat. rolls Ire., Chas I*, p. 331; Brian Mac Cuarta, 'The Irish revenues of Oliver St John, Viscount Grandison for 1625–9', *Analecta Hibernica*, 45 (2014), pp 149–206 at pp 151, 187–8.

42 *Cal. S.P. Ire., 1625–32*, p. 207.

43 J.C. Appleby and Mary O'Dowd, 'The Irish admiralty: its organization and development, c.1570–1640', *Irish Historical Studies*, 24:25 (1985), pp 299–326 at pp 307–21; St George to Lords of Admiralty, 30 Sept. 1635 (*Cal. S.P. Ire., 1633–47*, p. 111).

44 Inventory of the *Hope of Rouen*, Nov. 1627 (*Cal. S.P. Ire., 1625–32*, p. 311).

45 *Ir. rec. comm. rep. 1821–25*, p. 255.

46 Details of settlement relative to 1685 marriage of Catherine St George and Sir Edward Crofton, outlined in chancery bill filed by Crofton, 1694 (NAI, Thrift genealogical abstracts 13:3082).

47 Potter, 'Local government in Leitrim', p. 539.

48 W.A. Shaw, *The knights of England: a complete record from the earliest time to the present day of the knights of all the orders of chivalry in England, Scotland and Ireland, and of knights bachelors, incorporating a complete list of knights bachelors dubbed in Ireland* (2 vols, London, 1906), ii, p. 192.

49 *Cal. S.P. Ire., 1647–60*, p. 236.

50 Brendan Scott, 'Seventeenth-century Leitrim: plantation and rebellion' in Kelly and Scott (eds), *Leitrim history and society*, pp 279–96 at p. 289.

51 Francis Blundell to Lord Treasurer, no date in Treadwell (ed.), *Irish commission*, p. 46.

52 Depositions of John Winder (TCD, MS 831, fos 17r–17v); Anthony Milles (TCD, MS 831, fos 21r–22v); Gilbert Corbyn (MS 831, fos 28r–29v).

53 Deposition of Ann Frere (TCD, MS 830, fos 32r–33r).

54 Lords Justices to Council, 5 Nov. 1641 (*Ormonde MSS*, ii, p. 7); Lords Justices to Secretary Vane, 13 Nov. 1641 (*Cal. S.P. Ire., 1633–47*, p. 346).

55 Casway, 'The last lords of Leitrim', p. 573.

56 Deposition of James Stevenson (TCD MS 831, fos 48r–50v); Raymond Gillespie, 'Shaping Leitrim: local history and the worlds of Leitrim, 1670–1714' in

Kelly and Scott (eds), *Leitrim history and society*, pp 243–57 at p. 255.

57 Ibid.

58 Examinations of Hugh O'Connor (TCD, MS 831, fos 9r–9v); Conor O'Boyle (TCD, MS 831, fos 112r–113v).

59 Grant to George St George of castle and lands of Carrick, enrolled 25 Nov. 1637 (NAI, Lodge/5/392–3).

60 *A relation touching the present state and condition of Ireland collected by a committee of the House of Commons out of several letters lately come from the lords justice of Ireland* (London, 1641), pp 4–5.

61 Dominic Rooney, 'Sir Frederick Hamilton (1590–1647), Leitrim planter' in Kelly and Scott (eds), *Leitrim history and society*, pp 259–96 at pp 271–2.

62 Stevenson (TCD MS 831, fos 48r–50v).

63 Gillespie, *Seventeenth-century Ireland*, p. 157; *Orders made and established by the lords spiritual and temporal and the rest of the general assembly of the kingdome of Ireland met at the city of Kilkenny 24 Oct. 1642* (Kilkenny, 1642).

64 Ohlmeyer, *Making Ireland English*, p. 272.

65 *Life of James, duke of Ormond*, iii, pp 68, 170.

66 Ibid., ii, p. 262.

67 Stevenson (TCD MS 831, fo. 49v).

68 *Life of James, Duke of Ormond*, iii, p. 172.

69 J.T. Gilbert (ed.), *A contemporary history of affairs in Ireland, from AD1641–52* (3 vols, Dublin, 1879), i, p. 281.

70 Ibid., p. 31.

71 Treadwell (ed.), *Irish commission*, p. 675.

72 Richard Bellings, *History of the Irish Confederation and the war in Ireland, 1641–49*, ed. J.T. Gilbert (7 vols, Dublin, 1882–91), i, p. 52.

73 Lords Justices to Lord Lieutenant, 9 May 1642 (*Ormonde MSS*, ii, pp 124–5).

74 Nicholas Canny, 'The 1641 Depositions: a source for social and cultural history', *History Ireland*, 4:1(winter 1993), pp 52–5 at p. 53.

75 Sir G. Lane, 20 Apr. 1649 (*Ormonde MSS*, i, pp 127–8).

76 *A bloody fight in Ireland and a great victory obtained Charles Coote lord president of the province of Connacht against the British forces of Laggan* (London, 1649), p. 5.

77 Gillespie, *Seventeenth-century Ireland*, p. 182.

78 Ibid., p. 178.

79 Pádraig Lenihan, *Consolidating conquest: Ireland, 1603–1727* (Harlow, 2008), p. 132.

80 Clanricarde to Charles II, Drumruiske 27 Aug. 1651 (*Ormonde MSS*, i, p. 190).

81 Clanricarde to Lord Digby, 14 Oct. 1651 (*Ormonde MSS*, i, p. 219).

82 Mattimoe, *North Roscommon*, p. 124.

83 J.P. Prendergast, *The Cromwellian settlement of Ireland* (2nd ed., repr. 2014, London, 1870), p. 136; *Ormonde MSS*, iii, pp 420–1.

84 Act for the settling of Ireland (10 Aug. 1652).

85 W.J. Smyth, *Map-making, landscape and memory: a geography of colonial and early modern Ireland* (Cork, 2006), p. 181.

86 Ibid., p. 184.

87 Prendergast, *Cromwellian settlement*, p. 112.

88 John Cunningham, *Conquest and land in Ireland: the transplantation to Connacht, 1649–80* (Woodbridge, 2011), p. 110.

89 Ibid., pp 107, 110.

90 Prendergast, *Cromwellian settlement*, p. 94; Cunningham, *Conquest and land*, p. 116.

91 Smyth, *Map-making*, p. 184.

92 Prendergast, *Cromwellian settlement*, pp 205–6.

93 Raymond Gillespie, 'A question of survival: the O'Farrells and Longford in the seventeenth century' in Raymond Gillespie and Gerard Moran (eds), *Longford: essays in county history* (Dublin, 1991), pp 13–29 at p. 17; Seamus Pender (ed.), *A census of Ireland, circa 1659, with supplementary material from the poll money ordinances, 1660–61* (Dublin, 1939), pp 451–61.

94 W.J. Smyth suggests that the number of inhabitants should be multiplied by three to account for persons not liable for tax: Pender, *Census of Ireland*, c.1659 (Dublin, 1939, repr. 2002), intro, xv, xl.

95 Gillespie, *Seventeenth-century Ireland*, p. 216.

96 *Declaration of Charles Coote knight and baronet, lord president of Connacht and the rest of the council of officers of the army in Ireland present at Dublin, concerning the re-admission of the scheduled members* (Dublin, 1659/60), p. 7.

97 Essex to Arlington, 20, 25 Jan. 1672/3 (*Essex Papers, 1672–9*, ed. Osmund Airy (Camden, 1890), pp 50, 52).

98 King to Lords Justices, 21 Jan. 1661 (*Cal. S.P. Ire., 1660–2*, pp 188–9).

99 Shaw, *Knights of England*, pp 224, 230; *Burke's peerage, baronetage, knightage, clan chiefs and Scottish feudal barons* (107th ed. London, 2003), p. 3614.

100 Ohlmeyer, *Making Ireland English*, p. 52.

101 *His majesties gracious declaration for the settlement of the kingdome of Ireland, and satisfaction of the several interests of adventurers, soldiers and other his majesties subjects there* (Dublin, 1660), legally enacted in 14 and 15 Charles II, c. 2 [Ire.] (30 May 1662) and 17 and 18 Charles II, c. 2 [Ire.] (1665); *Ir. rec. comm. rep., 1821–5*, p. 31; *Cal. S.P. Ire., 1660–2*, p. 266.

102 K.S. Bottigheimer, 'The Restoration land settlement in Ireland: a structural view', *Irish Historical Studies*, 18:69 (Mar. 1972), pp 1–21 at p. 17.

103 O'Byrne, *Tyrone House*, p. 69.

104 *Ir. rec. comm. rep., 1821–5*, pp 78–9, 254–5; Simington, *Books of survey and distribution, Roscommon*, pp 30–4, 76–85, 132–54.

105 *Ir. rec. comm. rep., 1821–5*, p. 122.

106 Ohlmeyer, *Making Ireland English*, p. 308.

107 Grant of lands to Oliver St George under commission of grace, 1684, enrolled 9 Sept. 1685 (NAI, Lodge/8/655–8).

108 Lords Justices to Secretary Nicholas, 21 Aug. 1661 (*Cal. S.P. Ire., 1660–2*, p. 405).

109 Ibid., p. 407.

110 Ormond to Lords Justices, 24 Dec. 1661 (MS Carte 219, fo. 36); Ormond to Sir Arthur Forbes, 17 Feb. 1667 (MS Carte 163, fo. 55v).

111 Proclamation of the lord lieutenant, 25 June 1666 (*Cal. S.P. Ire., 1666–69*, p. 137).

112 Forbes to Page, 8 June 1666 (*Ormonde MSS*, iii, p. 225).

113 Lord Lieutenant to Arlington, 27 Feb. 1667 (*Cal. S.P. Ire., 1666–9*, p. 309); Perrott to Rawdon, 9 Mar. 1667 (*Cal. S.P. Ire., 1669–70*, p. 590).

114 *Life of James, duke of Ormond*, iv, p. 353.

115 *Cal. S.P. Ire., 1669–70*, pp 603–4.

116 *Essex Papers*, pp 266–8.

117 *Proclamation by the lord lieutenant general and general governor of Ireland* (Dublin,

1673); Memorandum Irish Privy Council, 30 Sept. 1679 (*Ormonde MSS*, v, pp 26–9).

118 Correspondence earls of Ormond and Arran, 13–15 Aug. 1681 (*Ormonde MSS*, vi, pp 132–3).

119 Rawdon to Conway, 17 Dec. 1666 (*Cal. S.P. Ire., 1666–9*, p. 257); Lord Lieutenant concerning subsidies, 11 Feb. 1666/7 (*Cal. S.P. Ire., 1666–9*, p. 297); 15 Chas II, c. 7 (1663); 18 Chas II, c. 2 [Ire.] (2 Feb. 1667).

120 St George v. St George (NLI, p4406).

121 Raymond Gillespie, *Colonial Ulster: the settlement of east Ulster, 1600–41* (Cork, 1985), p. 46.

122 Domhnall Mac an Ghallóglaigh, 'Leitrim, 1600–41', *Bréifne Journal*, 4:14 (1971), pp 225–54 at p. 232.

123 St George archive, Carrick-on-Shannon Historical Society. Access granted by kind permission of Mary Dolan; Donal O'Sullivan, *Carolan: the life, times and music of an Irish harper* (London, 1958), pp 31, 98.

124 St George v. St George (NLI, p4406).

125 Martin Dowling, *Traditional music and Irish society: historical perspectives* (London, 2014), pp 30–1.

126 James Hardiman, *Irish minstrelsy* (2 vols, London, 1831), i, p. xliii.

127 St George to Ormond, 15 Apr. 1685 (MS Carte 40, fo. 377).

128 An Act for the Attainder of Divers Rebels, and for Preserving the Interest of Loyal Subjects, 1689.

129 Mattimoe, *North Roscommon*, pp 132–5.

130 Mountjoy to Ormond, 17 July 1686 (*Ormonde MSS*, vii, p. 429); *Calendar of the Orrery Papers*, ed. Edward MacLysaght (Dublin, 1941), p. 372.

131 John Childs, *The Williamite wars in Ireland, 1688–91* (London, 2007), p. 26.

132 Childs, *Williamite wars*, pp 170, 311; Mattimoe, *North Roscommon*, p. 134.

133 Childs, *Williamite wars*, p. 27.

134 Ibid., p. 352.

135 Lenihan, *Consolidating conquest*, pp 188–9.

136 *Ir. rec. comm. rep. 1821–5*, p. 39.

137 *Iniquity displayed or the settlement of the kingdom of Ireland, commonly called, the Act of Settlement made after the restoration of King Charles II laid open 1667/8* (Dublin, 1704).

2. PAYING THE PRICE, 1691–1791

1   Toby Barnard, *Improving Ireland? Projectors, prophets and profiteers, 1641–1786* (Dublin, 2008), p. 15.

2   James Kelly (ed.), *The letters of Chief Baron Edward Willes to the earl of Warwick, 1757–62: an account of Ireland in the mid-eighteenth century* (Aberystwyth, 1990), p. 96.

3   Edited in James Carney, 'A tract on the O'Rourkes', *Celtica*, 1 (1946–50), pp 238–79 at p. 259.

4   21 & 22 Geo. III, c. 24 [Ire.] (4 May 1782).

5   St George v. St George (NLI, p4406).

6   Letters patent, 5 June 1715 (NLI, GO MS 161, p. 127).

7   Ohlmeyer, *Making Ireland English*, p. 5.

8   *Newcastle Courant*, 30 Aug. 1735.

9   Marriage settlement, Usher St George and Elizabeth Dominick, 17 July 1752 (RD, 159/59/105982); 'Dominick St.: why so-called?', *Irish Builder*, 37 (1895), p. 37.

10 Will of Lord St George, 1 Apr. 1773 (NAI, T/16845).

11 *Saunders's News-Letter*, 6 Nov. 1775; Terence Dooley, *The decline and fall of the dukes of Leinster, 1871–1948: love, war, debt and madness* (Dublin, 2014), p. 22.

12 Military appointments, Richard St George, 1690–1747 (NLI, D.22, 677–87).

13 St George pedigrees (NLI, GO MS 170).

14 W.P. Phillimore (ed.), *An index to changes of name under authority of act of parliament or royal licence, including irregular changes, 1760–1901* (London, 1905), p. xxi.

15 St George v. Bruen (NLI, MS 10,079); St George recovery, 22 Jan. 1747 (RD, 129/494/87959).

16 A.R. Maddison, *Lincolnshire pedigrees* (4 vols, London, 1906), iv, p. 1155; R.E. Waters, *Genealogical memoirs of the extinct family of Chester of Chicheley, their ancestors and descendants* (2 vols, London, 1878), ii, pp 674–95; St George pedigrees (NLI, GO MS 170).

17 *Pue's Occurrences*, 26 Aug. 1749.

18 Marriage settlement, Mary St George, 18 July 1749 (NAI, T/1025/3/28).

19 Geraldine Candon, *Headford, County Galway, 1775–1901* (Dublin, 2003), p. 10.

20 Will, Lieutenant General St George, 9 June 1753 (NA, UK, Prob. 11/924/262).

21 *Pue's Occurrences*, 26 July 1757.

22 St George v. Bruen (NLI, MS 10,079).

23 Dean of Westminster (ed.), *The remains of the late Mrs Richard Trench: being selections from her journals, letters and papers* (London, 1862), pp 13–14.

24 J.A. Venn (ed.), *Alumni Cantabrigienses* (10 vols, Cambridge, 1953), v, p. 399; *Hibernian Journal*, 16 Oct. 1778; *Saunders's News-Letter*, 18 Dec. 1780.

25 *Saunders's News-Letter*, 3 Nov. 1786.

26 *Dublin Evening Post*, 4 Aug. 1787.

27 Mortgage St George to Cope, 1 July 1783 (RD, 343/273/236047).

28 St George v. Bruen (NLI, MS 10,079); *Saunders's News-Letter*, 31 Aug. 1789.

29 *The Gentleman's Magazine and Historical Chronical for the Year 1790* (London, 1790), p. 372.

30 Baron of the exchequer to Ormond, George St George's house, Carrickdrumough, 25 Mar. 1706 (*Ormonde MSS*, viii, p. 226); St George to Roycroft, 25 Mar. 1713 (RD, 42/491/27148); St George to Eccles, 4 Oct. 1720 (RD, 28/412/18141).

31 Marriage settlement Judith Usher and George Lowther, 31 Mar. 1738 (RD, 91/35/63198).

32 Westminster (ed.), *Remains Mrs Trench*, p. 13.

33 William Wilson, *The Post-chaise companion; or, Travellers' directory through Ireland: to which is added a dictionary of alphabetical tables shewing the distance of all the principal cities, boroughs, market and seaport towns in Ireland from each other* (Dublin, 1786), p. 103.

34 William Robinson, 'The kingdom of Ireland with the distribution of the barracks for quartering the army 1700' in J.H. Andrews, *Shapes of Ireland: maps and their makers, 1564–1839* (Dublin, 1997), p. 158; D.A. Fleming, 'Military barracks in an age of revolt and war' in H.B. Clarke and Sarah Gearty (eds), *More maps and texts: sources and the Irish Historic Towns Atlas* (Dublin, 2018), pp 266–80 at p. 267.

35 10 Will. III. c. 6 [Ire.] (26 Jan. 1699); *Municipal corporations report*.

36 St George to Roycroft, 25 Mar. 1713 (RD, 42/491/27148). Provides an early legal record of the renaming of the town which pre-dates the first printed record identified as 1802: Nollaig Ó Muraíle, 'Place-names of County Leitrim' in Kelly and Scott (eds), *Leitrim history and society*, pp 311–35 at p. 324.

37 Herman Moll, *A new map of Ireland* (London, 1714); MacAtasney, *Plantation of Leitrim*, p. 61.
38 St George v. St George (NLI, p4406).
39 Ibid.
40 Gillespie, *Colonial Ulster*, p. 175.
41 Barnard, *Improving Ireland?*, p. 153.
42 St George to Eccles, 4 Oct. 1720 (RD, 28/412/18141).
43 Joyce to Gallagher, 20 Oct. 1729 (RD, 79/90/54732).
44 St George estate maps, 1768 (NLI, p2713).
45 Legg and Gurrin, *Census of Elphin, 1749*.
46 St George estate maps, 1768 (NLI, p2713).
47 Maps of the estate of Richard St George Mansergh St George, 1775 (NLI, microfilm, p5483), available at www.galway.ie/digitalarchives, last accessed 11 Apr. 2023.
48 Ibid.
49 Kelly (ed.), *Letters of Chief Baron Edward Willes*, p. 93.
50 Ibid.
51 An account of Headford, Galway, by Richard St George Mansergh St George, c.1790 (TCD, MS 1749), https://digitalcollections.tcd.ie (accessed 11 Apr. 2023).
52 Ibid.
53 Kelly (ed.), *Letters of Chief Baron Edward Willes*, p. 93.
54 Ibid.
55 Bernard Scalé, *Hibernian atlas; or, General description of the kingdom of Ireland* (Dublin, 1776), not paginated.
56 Maps of the estate of R. Mansergh St George, 1775 (NLI, microfilm, p5483); Headford, c.1790 (TCD, MS 1749).
57 Dooley, *Decline of the dukes of Leinster*, p. 22.
58 *Dublin Evening Post*, 18 Sept. 1790.
59 Ibid.
60 J.S. Tiedemann, 'Patriots by default: Queens County, New York and the British Army, 1776–83', *William and Mary Quarterly*, 43:1 (Jan. 1986), pp 35–63 at pp 43–4.
61 St George to Bruen, 1 Dec. 1783 (RD 358/209/239741).
62 CRO to John Keogh (RD 450/116/289254).
63 CRO to John McLoughlin (RD 446/31/286981).
64 CRO to Gilbert Roycroft for John McLoughlin (RD 442/149/287960).
65 CRO to Hugh O'Beirne (RD 444/306/288751).
66 *Dublin Evening Post*, 19 Apr. 1785.
67 Charles Coote to Hugh O'Beirne, 20 Apr. 1822 (RD 771/403/522938).
68 CRO to John Farrell (RD 436/540/283113); CRO to Edward Kelly (RD 438/410/283111); CRO to Luke Kilmartin (RD 517/158/339332).
69 CRO to Robert French (RD 436/543/283119).
70 CRO to Peter La Touche (RD 438/96/282002).
71 CRO to John King (RD 437/374/283112); CRO to Thomas Lloyd (RD 437/377/283115); CRO to Robert Guff (RD 438/414/283114); CRO to Reynolds Peyton (RD 441/197/289166); CRO to Robert Duke (RD 437/373/283109); CRO to William Phibbs (RD 438/410/283108).
72 Maureen Wall, 'The rise of the Catholic middle class in eighteenth-century Ireland', *Irish Historical Studies*, 11:42 (Sept. 1958), pp 91–115 at pp 110–11.

3. THE RISE OF THE CATHOLIC COMMUNITY, 1791–1830

1 Venn, *Alumni Cantabrigienses*, p. 399; Edward Hertslet (ed.), *The Foreign Office list, forming a complete British diplomatic and consular handbook* (London, 1865), p. 143.
2 Ratification marriage Charles and Ingri St George, 10 Aug. 1833, St Marylebone parish registers.
3 *Full and accurate report of the debates in the parliament of Ireland in the session 1793 on the bill for the relief of his majesty's Catholic subjects* (Dublin, 1793), pp xv, xxiii.
4 Eamon O'Flaherty, 'The Catholic Convention and Anglo-Irish politics', *Archivium Hibernicum*, 45 (1985), pp 14–34 at p. 28; 32 Geo. III, c. 21 [Ire.] (18 Apr. 1793).
5 33 Geo. III, c. 29 [Ire.] (7 Aug. 1793); 33 Geo. III, c. 22 [Ire.] (9 Apr. 1793).
6 Thomas Bartlett, 'Select documents, xxxviii: Defenders and Defenderism in 1795', *Irish Historical Studies*, 24:95 (May 1985), pp 373–94 at pp 374–6.
7 Col. Craddock, Carrick, 29 May 1793 (PRO, London, HO 100/44/7) cited in Kelly, *Rebels and Frenchmen in Leitrim, 1793–98*, p. 25.

8 *Dublin Evening Post*, 6 Sept. 1794.

9 E. Newenham, Carrick, undated 1795 (NAI, CSO, RP 620/22/19).

10 Mr Fearns, Carrick 20 Apr. 1795 (NAI, CSO, RP 620/22/19).

11 E. Newenham, Carrick, 18 Apr. 1795 (NAI, CSO, RP 620/22/19).

12 Bartlett, 'Defenders and Defenderism', p. 382.

13 Kelly, *Rebels and Frenchmen*, p. 38.

14 Mr Murphy to Dublin Castle, Carrick, 20 Apr. 1795 (PRO, HO 100/58/193–81), transcribed in Bartlett, 'Defenders and Defenderism', p. 382.

15 *Faulkner's Dublin Journal*, 5 May 1795.

16 *Hibernian Journal or Chronicle of Liberty*, 15 May 1795.

17 Kelly, *Rebels and Frenchmen*, pp 49–50.

18 J.L. Jobit, 'Journal de l'expédition d'Irlande suivi sur le Général Humbert qui l'a commandé', *Analecta Hibernica*, 11 (July 1941), pp 5–55 at p. 12.

19 *Kentish Gazette*, 31 Aug. 1798.

20 W.H. Maxwell, *History of the Irish rebellion in 1798* (London, 1845), p. 240.

21 *Impartial relation of the military operations which took place in Ireland in consequence of the landing of a body of French troops, under General Humbert, in August 1798* (Dublin, 1799), p. 67.

22 *A concise history of the rebellion in Ireland which broke out in the month of May 1798; together with an account of all the battles that have been fought between the king's troops and insurgents* (Liverpool, 1798), p. 66.

23 Jobit, 'Journal de l'expédition', pp 32–3.

24 'MS journal of a field officer' transcribed in Maxwell, *Irish rebellion*, pp 243–4.

25 *Manuscripts duke of Buccleuch and Queensbury*, i, p. 76.

26 Letter Revd Mr Collis discussing the murder of Richard St George Mansergh St George, 16 Feb. 1798 (TCD, MS 1749).

27 *Military operations, 1798*, p. 40.

28 Westminster (ed.), *Remains Mrs Trench*, p. 33.

29 Duke Crofton to Lord Clements, 10 Feb. 1799 (NLI Killadoon Papers, MS 36,061/2).

30 James Kelly, 'Politics in Ireland and the Act of Union', *Transactions of the Royal Historical Society*, 10 (2000), pp 259–87 at p. 279; Myles Keon, Carrick to Lord Castlereagh, 8 Jan. 1800 in Charles Vane (ed.), *Memoirs and correspondence of Viscount Castlereagh, second marquess of Londonderry* (12 vols, London, 1848–53), iii, p. 222.

31 Keon to Castlereagh in Vane, *Memoirs of Viscount Castlereagh*, iii, pp 222–3.

32 *Dublin Evening Post*, 29 Apr. 1806.

33 Hugh O'Beirne to Lord Clements, 24 Dec. 1801 (NLI, Killadoon Papers, MS 36,061/4).

34 *Dublin Evening Post*, 20 Feb. 1817.

35 Wakefield, *Account of Ireland*, ii, p. 614.

36 Hugh O'Beirne to Lord Leitrim, 4 Nov. 1812 (NLI, Killadoon Papers, MS 36,061/8).

37 Francis O'Beirne to London Tavern Committee (LTC), 23 July 1822, *Report of the committee for the relief of the distressed districts in Ireland, appointed at the City of London Tavern on the 7th of May 1822* (London, 1823), p. 82 (henceforth *LTC report*).

38 *First report from the select committee on the state of disease and condition of the labouring poor in Ireland*, pp 49, 58, HC 1819 (314), viii, 413, 422.

39 C.M. St George to Robert Robinson, 28 June 1827, citing earlier lease (RD, 1833/6/34).

40 *LTC report*, p. 8.

41 Francis O'Beirne, 4 Oct. 1822, *LTC report*, p. 68.

42 Resolutions of relief meeting held at Kiltohart [*sic*], 29 May 1822, photographically reproduced courtesy of the Guildhall Library, London, in MacAtasney, *The other famine*, pp 81–2.

43 *Roscommon and Leitrim Gazette*, 13 July 1822.

44 Francis O'Beirne, 4 Oct. 1822, *LTC report*, p. 68.

45 St George to Cox, 13 Oct. 1834 (RD, 1837/9/116).

46 Candon, *Headford*, p. 15.

47 MacAtasney, *The other famine*, pp 107–8.

48 Ibid., p. 121.

49 Hyett, 3 Sept. 1822, *LTC report*, p. 111.

50 Leitrim Central Committee, Carrick, 2 Sept. 1822, *LTC report*, p. 180.

51 George Waddington, 12 Sept. 1822, *LTC report*, p. 132.

52 *Enniskillen Chronicle*, 1 June 1826.

53 *Roscommon and Leitrim Gazette*, 22 Sept. 1827.

54 James McParlan, *Statistical survey of County Leitrim with observations on the means of improvement: drawn up for consideration by order of the Dublin Society* (Dublin, 1802), p. 45.

55 Francis O'Beirne, 23 Jan. 1823 cited in MacAtasney, *The other famine*, p. 196.

56 *Westmeath Journal*, 13 Nov. 1823.

57 *Dublin Evening Mail*, 8 Nov. 1824.

58 *Dublin Evening Mail*, 8 Nov. 1824; *Dublin Morning Register*, 16 Nov. 1824.

59 *Saunders's News-letter*, 23 Apr. 1823; *Accounts and papers relative to schools and education in Ireland*, pp 72–3, HL 1824 (134), clxix, pp 72–3.

60 *First report of the commission on education in Ireland*, p. 485, HC 1825 (400), xii, p. 601.

61 *Dublin Morning Register*, 13 Feb. 1826.

62 *Roscommon and Leitrim Gazette*, 13 May 1826.

63 Proinnsíos Ó Duigneáin, 'The public career of Rev. Thomas Maguire, 1792–1847' in Kelly and Scott (eds), *Leitrim history and society*, pp 495–514 at p. 499.

64 *Second report of the commissioners of Irish education inquiry*, pp 1198–9, HC 1826–7 (12), xii, p. 4.

65 *Dublin Weekly Register*, 15 Sept. 1827.

66 Ibid., 29 Sept. 1827.

67 Hugh Walsh to Lord Leitrim (NLI, Killadoon Papers, MS 36,061/14).

68 Insp. George Warburton to CSO, 17–25 Jan. 1828 (NAI, CSO/RP/1828/631–2).

69 *Westmeath Journal*, 6 Nov. 1828.

70 *Dublin Evening Post*, 4 Nov. 1828.

71 Fergus O'Ferrall, 'The emergence of the political community in Longford, 1824–29' in Gillespie and Moran (eds), *Longford essays*, pp 123–51 at p. 138.

72 *Roscommon and Leitrim Gazette*, 24 Jan. 1829.

73 Ibid., 17 Jan 1829.

74 10 Geo. IV, c. 7 [Ire.] (13 Apr. 1829).

75 D.R. Fisher (ed.), *The history of parliament: House of Commons 1830–32* (7 vols, Cambridge, 2009), History of Parliament, www.historyofparliament online.org (23 Sept. 2022).

76 *Westmeath Journal*, 25 Mar. 1830.

77 *Roscommon and Leitrim Gazette*, 22 Jan. 1831; 30 Apr. 1831.

78 *Freeman's Journal*, 12 May 1831.

79 Roscommon *and Leitrim Gazette*, 13 Feb. 1830; Meehan, 'High sheriffs, Leitrim', p. 386.

80 *Roscommon and Leitrim Gazette*, 14 May 1831.

81 *London Courier and Evening Gazette*, 19 May 1831.

82 W.P. Percy to Lord Clements, 19 July 1801 (NLI Killadoon Papers, MS 36,061/23).

83 *Belfast Commercial Chronicle*, 24 Dec. 1806.

84 *Papers relating to the internal judicature of Ireland, 1786–1819*, pp 52–5, HC 1819–20 (15), iii, pp 352–5; *Belfast Commercial Chronicle*, 20 Mar. 1811; Wakefield, *Account of Ireland*, ii, p. 334.

85 *A return of the names of places where barracks and barrack establishments are kept for the army in Ireland*, p. 2, HC 1822 (291), xviii, p. 434; *Accounts relating to barracks in Ireland: summary account of all works and buildings that have been or are now carrying on: list of permanent barracks: list of the several temporary barracks*, p. 7, HC 1812–3 (237), vi, p. 715; *Return of such temporary barracks in charge of Barrack Dept. in Ireland, as appear to have been hired between 1st of Aug. 1813 and 1st Feb. 1816, for the occupancy of military parties to assist the officers of excise in seizing unlicensed stills*, p. 1, HC 1816 (182), ix, p. 407.

86 Wakefield, *Account of Ireland*, ii, pp 614, 621.

87 3 Geo. IV, c. 103 [UK] (5 Aug. 1822).

88 *Kilkenny Moderator*, 6 Dec. 1828.

89 *Roscommon and Leitrim Gazette*, 28 July 1827, 19 July 1828; Andrew Johnston to CSO, 16 Oct. 1829 (NAI, CSO/RP/1829/419).

90 *Roscommon and Leitrim Gazette*, 1 Mar. 1828.

91 Warburton to CSO, 20 Feb. 1828 (NAI, CSO/RP/1828/643): Warburton to CSO, 12–20 Apr. 1828 (NAI, CSO/RP/1828/671); Captain Shafto, 12th Regiment Carrick to CSO, 13 June 1828 (NAI, CSO/RP/1828/674).

92 Warburton to CSO, 10 Mar. 1828 (NAI, CSO/RP/1828/651).

93 *Enniskillen Chronicle*, 17 Jan. 1828.

94 Reynolds Irwin to CSO, 24 Apr. 1826 (NAI, CSO/RP/1826/567).

95 *Dublin Evening Packet*, 5 Aug. 1828.

96 Captain Charles Cox and George Peyton to Chief Secretary, Carrick, 3 Dec. 1829 (NAI, CSO/1829/120/3).

97 McParlan, *Statistical survey of Co. Leitrim*, pp 65, 69, 71.

98 Ibid., p. 33.
99 Potter, 'Local government in Leitrim',
p. 539.
100 McParlan, *Statistical survey of Co.
Leitrim*, pp 46, 68.
101 *Saunders's News-Letter*, 27 Dec. 1803.
102 McParlan, *Statistical survey of Co.
Leitrim*, p. 66.
103 *Walker's Magazine; or, Compendium
of entertaining knowledge* (Nov. 1807),
pp 675–80 at pp 677–8.
104 Ibid.
105 Ibid.
106 James Hall, *A tour through Ireland:
particularly the interior and least known
parts* (2 vols, London, 1813), ii, p. 35.
107 *Abstract of the answers and returns made
pursuant to an act of the united parliament,
passed in the 55th year of the reign of his
late majesty George III, intitled, An Act
to Provide for Taking an Account of the
Population of Ireland, and for Ascertaining
the Increase and Diminution thereof,
Preliminary Observations, Enumeration
Abstract,* appendix, pp 342–3, HC 1824
(577), xxii, pp 776–7.
108 Lord Leitrim to Lady Leitrim,
24 Feb. 1826 (NLI, Killadoon Papers,
36.034/11).
109 *Dublin Evening Post*, 18 Jan. 1810;
Ambrose Leet, *A directory to the market
towns, villages and gentlemen's seats and
other noted places in Ireland* (2nd ed.,
Dublin, 1814), p. 215.
110 Hely Dutton, *Statistical and agricultural
survey of the county of Galway* (Dublin,
1824), pp 330–1.
111 *Roscommon and Leitrim Gazette*, 22 Sept.
1827.

4. 'IT IS FINISHED', 1830–64
1 *Roscommon and Leitrim Gazette*, 15 May
1830.
2 Ibid., 22 Sept. 1827, 22 May 1830.
3 Childs, *Williamite wars*, p. 293.
4 St George to Lord Leitrim, 16 May 1830
(NLI, Killadoon Papers, MS 36,061/16).
5 Samuel White, Carrick to Lord Leitrim,
25 Aug. 1830 (NLI, Killadoon Papers MS
36,061/17).
6 *Thom's Irish almanac and official directory,*
1849–64.
7 *Roscommon Journal and Western Impartial
Reporter*, 3 Sept. 1836.

8 *Roscommon and Leitrim Gazette*, 27 Aug.
1836.
9 Ibid., 22 Oct. 1836.
10 Robert Cox to St George, 25 Jan. 1849
(RD, 1849/5/151).
11 *Roscommon and Leitrim Gazette*, 7 Aug. 1841.
12 Ibid., 28 Apr. 1838.
13 *The Pilot*, 24 June 1839.
14 *Roscommon and Leitrim Gazette*, 22 June
1839.
15 *Dublin Evening Post*, 2 June 1839.
16 *Municipal corporations report.*
17 *Roscommon and Leitrim Gazette*, 2 June
1832 and 9 Nov. 1844.
18 Ibid., 8 Apr. 1837.
19 Ibid., 17 June 1837.
20 *Fifth report of the commissioners appointed
pursuant to the Act 5 and 6 Will. IV. c. 67 for
the improvement of the navigation of the River
Shannon; with an appendix,* 4 [173], HC
1839, xxviii, p. 142.
21 *Dublin Evening Post*, 29 Nov. 1838, 11 Jan.
1845.
22 St George to Lord Leitrim, 24 Apr. 1844
(NLI, Killadoon Papers, MS 36,060/7).
23 *Slater's national commercial directory of
Ireland* (Manchester, 1846), p. 112.
24 *Gardeners' Chronicle and Agricultural
Gazette*, 13 Sept. 1845.
25 Cormac Ó Gráda, *Black '47 and beyond the
Great Irish Famine in history and economic
memory* (Princeton, 1999), p. 49.
26 1 & 2 Vic., c. 56 (3 July 1838).
27 *Appendix to minutes of evidence taken
before select committee of the House of Lords
appointed to inquire into the operation of the
1st and 2nd Vict. cap. 56 and the laws relating
to the relief of the destitute poor in Ireland; and
also to inquire into the operation of medical
charities in Ireland which are supported by
grants from county cess,* p. 375, HC 1846
(694–ii), xi pt ii, p. 397.
28 St George to Poor-Law Commissioners,
4 Dec. 1839 and 22 May 1849 (RD,
1839/23/59 and 1850/17/18).
29 Viscount Clements to Relief
Commission, 22 Mar. 1846 (NAI, RLFC
3/1/873).
30 Appointment of relief committee
for the Carrick district, 3 Apr. 1846,
photographically reproduced, courtesy
of St George's Heritage Centre, Carrick,
in MacAtasney, *Great Famine in Leitrim*,
p. 74.

31 *Seventh annual report of the commissioners for the improvement of the navigation of the River Shannon, Ireland: with an appendix*, p. 2, HC 1846 (153), xxii, p. 464.

32 *Sixth annual report of the commissioners for the improvement of the navigation of the River Shannon, Ireland: with an appendix*, p. 2, HC 1845 (178), xxvi, p. 368.

33 *Eighth annual report of the commissioners for the improvement of the navigation of the River Shannon, Ireland: with an appendix*, p. 33, HC 1847 (545), xvii, p. 644.

34 9 & 10 Vic., c. 1–4 (5 Mar. 1846).

35 *Tenth annual report of the commissioners for the improvement of the navigation of the River Shannon, Ireland: with an appendix*, p. 25, HC 1849 (113), xxiii, p. 761; *Correspondence explanatory of the measures adopted by her majesty's government for the relief of distress arising from the failure of the potato crop in Ireland*, 368 [735], HC 1846, xxxvii, p. 420 (henceforth *Relief arising from failure of potato crop*).

36 *Correspondence from July 1846 to January 1847 relating to the measures adopted for the relief of distress in Ireland, Board of Works series*, 140, 164, 445 [764], HC 1847, l, pp 160, 184, 473 (henceforth *Relief of distress, Board of Works, July 1846–Jan. 1847*).

37 *Relief arising from failure of the potato crop*, 203 [735], HC 1846, xxxvii, p. 256.

38 10 Vic., c. 7 (26 Feb. 1847).

39 *Distress (Ireland) supplementary appendix to the seventh and last report of the relief commissioners constituted under the act 10th Vic., cap. 7*, 18 [956], HC 1847–8, xxix, p. 138.

40 Revd Dawson to Commissioners, 11 Dec. 1847, *Papers relating to proceedings for the relief of the distress and the state of the unions and workhouses in Ireland, fifth series*, 139 [919], HC 1847–8, lv, p. 167 (henceforth *State of the unions and workhouses, fifth series*).

41 10 Vic. c. 31 (8 June 1847); 10 & 11 Vic. c. 90 (22 July 1847).

42 Commissioners to Poor-Law inspector, Capt. Wynne, 31 Dec. 1847, *State of the unions and workhouses, fifth* series, 153 [919], HC 1847–8, lv, p. 181.

43 Wynne to Commissioners, 27 Nov. 1847, *State of the unions and workhouses, fifth* series, 141 [919], HC 1847–8, lv, p. 169.

44 9 & 10 Vic., c. 1–4 (5 Mar. 1846).

45 Commissioners to Wynne, 8 Dec. 1847, *State of the unions and workhouses, fifth* series, 144 [919], HC 1847–8, lv, p. 172; *Papers relating to proceedings for the relief of distress and the state of the unions and workhouses in Ireland, sixth series*, 734 [955], HC 1847–8, lvi, p. 772.

46 *Poor Law (Ireland). Abstract of returns of each Poor-Law union in Ireland, specifying the electoral divisions and the valuation thereof; rates made during the year ended 25 March 1848 and amount thereof*, p. 36, HC 1847–8 (707), liii, p. 590.

47 Wynne to Commissioners, 13 Aug. 1848, *Papers relating to proceedings for the relief of the distress and the state of the unions and workhouses in Ireland, seventh* series, 23 [999], HC 1847–8, liv, p. 343.

48 *Leitrim Journal*, 1 Sept. 1853.

49 St George rentals 1842–71 (NLI, MS 4001–MS 4022), not paginated.

50 Ibid., 1846 and 1850 (NLI, MS 4005, MS 4006).

51 *Leitrim Journal*, 1 May 1851.

52 *Leitrim Observer*, 15 July 1950.

53 MacAtasney, *Great Famine in Leitrim*, p. 304.

54 St George to Bourns, 10 June 1841, reciting deed dated 10 July 1780 (RD, 1841/15/134).

55 MacAtasney, *Great Famine in Leitrim*, p. 179; St George 1851 rentals (NLI, MS 4007).

56 *Roscommon and Leitrim Gazette*, 31 Oct. 1846; St George 1851 rentals (NLI, MS 4007).

57 Robinson v. Kean, 13 Aug. 1849, Foster v. Gray, 7 May 1849 (NAI, Carrick Petty Sessions order books, CSPS 3/003).

58 *King's County Chronicle*, 11 Apr. 1849.

59 Guardians Carrick Union v. O'Reilly and others, 7 May 1849 (NAI, Carrick Petty Sessions order books, CSPS 3/003).

60 St George 1846 rentals, 1846 (NLI, MS 4005).

61 *Slater's royal national commercial directory of Ireland, Connacht* (Manchester, 1870), p. 21.

62 Tunny v. McGaherty, 15 Dec. 1849 (NAI, Carrick Petty Sessions order books, CSPS 3/032).

63 Rogers v. O'Connor, 7 Dec. 1849 (NAI, Carrick Petty Sessions order books, CSPS 3/003).

64 *Relief of distress, Board of Works, July 1846–Jan. 1847*, 323 [764], HC 1847, l, p. 351.

65 *Banner of Ulster*, 16 Mar. 1849; Robinson v. Carr, 8 July 1850 (NAI, Carrick Petty Sessions order books, CSPS 3/003).

66 *Correspondence from January to March 1847 relating to the measures adopted for the relief of distress in Ireland, Board of Works series*, 122 [797], HC 1847, lii, p. 132.

67 *Saunder's News-Letter*, 18 July 1846; St George 1846 rentals (NLI, MS 4005).

68 *Freeman's Journal*, 6 Mar. 1848; *Cork Examiner*, 10 Mar. 1848.

69 St George 1846 rentals (NLI, MS 4005).

70 St George 1851 rentals (NLI, MS 4006).

71 *Freeman's Journal*, 9 Oct. 1849.

72 *Roscommon and Leitrim Gazette*, 26 Dec. 1846.

73 St George Carrick estate, payments and allowances made to tenants for building and drainage and estate expenditure from year 1850 (NLI, MS 4073).

74 St George 1851 rentals (NLI, MS 4007).

75 *Dublin Weekly Register*, 5 Jun. 1847; *Sligo Champion*, 21 Aug. 1847.

76 Carrick payments and allowances (NLI, MS 4073).

77 Cox to St George, 25 Jan. 1849 (RD, 1849/5/151).

78 *Thom's Irish almanac* (Dublin, 1851), p. 1851.

79 *Census of Ireland for the year 1851*, part vi, *general report*, xiv [2134], HC 1856, xxxi, p. 14.

80 *Dublin Evening Mail*, 24 May 1847.

81 Candon, *Headford*, p. 16.

82 *Dublin Evening Packet*, 23 Sept. 1851.

83 *Roscommon and Leitrim Gazette*, 15 Nov. 1851.

84 Carrick payments and allowances (NLI, MS 4073), p. 48; Thomas Lacey, *Sights and scenes in our fatherland* (London, 1863), pp 300–1.

85 *Dublin Evening packet*, 22 June 1852; *Leitrim Journal*, 29 July 1852.

86 *The Evening Freeman*, 22 June 1852.

87 13 & 14 Vic., c. 69 [Ire.] (14 Aug. 1850); Liam McNiff, 'The Leitrim election of 1852' in Kelly and Scott (eds), *Leitrim history and society*, pp 473–93 at pp 476–7.

88 11 & 12 Vic., c. 48 [Ire.].

89 *Freeman's Journal*, 23 July 1852; *Roscommon and Leitrim Gazette*, 14 Aug. 1852.

90 McNiff, 'Leitrim election 1852', p. 486.

91 *Leitrim Journal*, 29 July 1852.

92 St George to Leitrim Conservatives, 28 July 1852, *Leitrim Journal*, 29 July 1852.

93 *Leitrim Journal*, 29 July 1852.

94 *Kerry Evening Post*, 9 Oct. 1852; *Evidence taken before Her Majesty's commissioners of inquiry into the state of endowed schools in Ireland, i*, 331 [2336–ii], HC 1857–8, xxii pt. ii, p. 339.

95 *Catholic Telegraph*, 24 Dec. 1852.

96 *Roscommon and Leitrim Gazette*, 15 Jan. 1853; *Freeman's Journal*, 31 Jan. 1853.

97 *Leitrim Journal*, 1 Sept. 1853.

98 *Dublin Evening Post*, 23 Sept. 1851; St George to l'Herault, 11 Sept. 1858, 28 Sept. 1863 (RD, 1858/28/279, 1863/32/82).

99 *Waterford Chronicle*, 18 Feb. 1860.

100 *Roscommon and Leitrim Gazette*, 12 Apr. 1862.

101 Tenants' address and St George's response, *Roscommon and Leitrim Gazette*, 8 Aug. 1863.

102 Ibid.

103 Lacey, *Sights and scenes*, pp 300–1.

104 Burials C.M. St George and Ingri St George, 13 May 1865, 24 Apr. 1873 (RCB Library, Kiltoghert Church of Ireland Parish Register); Calendar of Wills and Administrations, 1858–1920, pp 318, 619, NAI, www.willcalendars.nationalarchives.ie/search/cwa/home.jsp (12 Oct. 2022).

105 Carrick payments and allowances (NLI, MS 4073), p. 48.

106 St George memorial, St George's Church, Carrick; *Roscommon and Leitrim Gazette*, 12 Sept. 1868.

CONCLUSION

1 *Manuscripts duke of Buccleuch and Queensberry*, i, p. 76.

2 Ibid., p. 75.

3 Noble, *College of arms*, p. 236.

4 Lawrence Stone, *The crisis of the aristocracy, 1558–1641* (London, 1965), pp 23, 120.

5 Ohlmeyer, *Making Ireland English*, p. 478.

6 O'Byrne, *Tyrone House*, p. 69.

7 *Roscommon and Leitrim Gazette*, 8 Aug. 1863.

Index